Principal of Léonie Cowen & Associates, Léonie is a recognised expert with an extensive track record. She has a 'can do' approach based on a deep understanding of how to achieve successful outcomes despite legislative constraints. She is renowned for her skill in advising on delivery of successful commissioning and procurement (particularly for children's and adults services, leisure and cultural services), achieving sustainable social enterprise and commercial models (including LATCOs/Teckal companies). Recently, she has advised extensively on the meaning and impact of the Public Contract Regulations 2016 and Concession Contracts Regulations 2016 and how to deliver effective procured outcomes especially for "light touch" services. She is currently advising on the impact of COVID-19 on local authority leisure contracts.

A Practical Guide to Local Authority Leisure Contracts in England and Wales in the Time of Covid-19, Brexit and Beyond

A Practical Guide to Local Authority Leisure Contracts in England and Wales in the Time of Covid-19, Brexit and Beyond

Léonie Cowen
Solicitor and Principal of Léonie Cowen & Associates

Law Brief Publishing

Published 2021 by Law Brief Publishing, an imprint of Law Brief Publishing Ltd
30 The Parks
Minehead
Somerset
TA24 8BT

www.lawbriefpublishing.com

Paperback: 978-1-913715-53-3

To my husband, Andrew Riddell with

thanks for all his support at home and work

over more than 30 years and to my

daughter, Eloise for brightening my life!

PREFACE

This short book is intended to be a practical handbook for busy legal practitioners. Whilst aimed at lawyers it should also be of interest and value to commissioners and procurement officers, leisure professionals, financial and other central support officers in local government the private and voluntary sectors.

The book sets out a brief history of leisure and culture externalisation focussing more extensively on leisure as this is by far the larger procurement market. It sets out a résumé of the current legal, procurement and commercial issues which local authorities and their providers or contractors should take into account when re-procuring leisure and culture, procuring for the first time. It also includes the legal and related considerations to be considered when managing relationships with their current provider.

Whilst in practice, new arrangements are likely to be via a procured contractual approach, alternative models of service delivery for leisure and recreation services are also identified because there are many of these still in existence and will be for some years and because there are alternative approaches which are used.

The book is written on the assumption that readers will use it as a practical guide. Chapters are therefor cross referred to each other. There is also some repetition to allow a reader to understand a topic without having to keep going back to the chapter where it is explained in detail. By way of explanation of the language used in this book. A provider is any third party which delivers a leisure or culture service. It is wider than the expression contractor. A contractor is a third-party organisation which delivers services pursuant to a procured or negotiated contract. Both expressions are commonly used in this marketplace. When discussing procurement processes the expression bidder is used rather than tenderer.

Whilst as identified, the primary focus of this book is indoor leisure, it also includes some consideration of:

- outdoor leisure and sports development;

- libraries; and

- other cultural activities such as theatres and museums.

These are all mentioned to acknowledge the commercial reality, that some local authorities have multi-service portfolios within their internal culture departments, though not usually including libraries. A local authority may well want to externalise all or most of these services as this makes operational sense. Whether it makes sense to the market will depend on the portfolio.

Whilst there is considerable available guidance from trade associations and other on externalisation including consideration of how to deliver an externalisation together with a description of all possible delivery models there is limited available guidance on the legal and procurement issues which local authorities and their partner should consider when entering into third party contracts for these services. This book's purpose is to fill this gap not to cover ground already covered in this guidance.

The scope of this book is English and Welsh law and law which is common to the four United Kingdom countries. The public procurement regime is currently identical across England, Wales and Northern Ireland. There are minor differences in Scotland. Law specific to Scotland and Northern Ireland is not within scope.

The known and likely implications of COVID-19 are included within this book to the extent that they are understood at present. However, these are still emerging and it is envisaged will take some months or even longer to become clear. These will not be clearer until there are a significant number of projects procured post the commencement of the pandemic. Whilst it is appreciated that at the time of writing there are a number of government and other grant initiatives to support local authorities and providers these are not identified and considered as they are transitory.

The book is up to date as at 24th January 2021.

Many thanks are given to Rachel Fowler of Strategic Leisure Limited, who has read and commented on the book and whose assistance has been invaluable.

Léonie Cowen
January 2021

CONTENTS

CHAPTER ONE

HISTORY OF LOCAL AUTHORITY LEISURE CONTRACTS AND CURRENT PROVISION

Introduction

In this chapter the following will be considered:

- the Beginnings of local authority leisure;

- compulsory Competitive Tendering and the Development of the local authority trust;

- the Legacy of the Past and the Current Marketplace

The Beginnings of Local Authority Leisure Facilities

Publicly funded and delivered sport and leisure services are nearly 200 years old. Legislative and charitable initiatives were developed from the latter part of the nineteenth century to address health issues, poverty and poor social conditions for example by the Baths and Washhouses Act 1846 and later legislation introducing initiatives to enable poorer people to bathe and later to swim. The Public Health Act 1875, Open Spaces Act 2006 and Public Health Act 1936 which allowed local authorities to provide baths, bathing spaces and washhouses are all still partly in force. Between them these acts developed the concepts that health, cleanliness and exercise are good for people acknowledging that many people did not have any access in their homes to bathing facilities. Initiatives to add parks and open spaces as areas for public walks and healthy outdoor games, enabling land to be taken into public ownership and maintained by local government for the benefit of the community were encouraged. Current legislation regulating local authority leisure and disposal powers have their history in these and later acts of parliament, the Physical

Training and Recreation Act 1937 and Local Government Act 1938. A number of existing leisure centres and facilities are wholly or partly on sites which came into public ownership in the nineteenth and early twentieth century and/or are built on public open space land. There are even some existing historic nineteenth (?) century buildings still used as leisure centres.

In parallel with the growth of public sector leisure and recreation there was a philanthropic growth in donations of land or charitable funds which funded the purchase of recreational land for open air activities or the building of leisure centres. Some of this recreational land has since come into local authority ownership often without a revenue endowment to support management.

The Education Acts of 1918 and 1944 included the provision of facilities for sport and recreation by local government, made mandatory in 1944 and currently swimming and water safety are part of the national curriculum for primary school children in both England and Wales. In the nineteen sixties government funding and initiatives meant the building of dual use facilities (built on education land but also used by the community) and joint use facilities (possibly built on school land but funded by both education and leisure authorities). Schools and the local authorities responsible for recreation and leisure shared responsibility for maintaining and providing these dual or join use facilities with use for the community outside school hours.

Whilst these arrangements ought to have been reflected in a formal dual use agreement with transparent identification of the respective times of use, cost allocation and relationship with a management body in place in practice, this is not always the case. Any formal written documents are usually out of date, ignored in part or in whole with relationships on the ground depending on the personalities involved. Many of these facilities remain today. Recent tensions around health and safety and safeguarding because of access for the public from within a school site and/or shared changing facilities has created difficulty and when schools are re-built there is separation.

As part of the schools re-building programmes within the private finance initiative ("PFI") or other government initiatives many schools have included modern fully leisure facilities including water. These may or may not be managed by the PFI contractor, procured separately by the school or relevant local authority, e.g. as part of a wider leisure contract or managed directly by the school with limited community access.

In parallel with this was legislation setting up national parks and areas of outstanding natural beauty under the National Parks and Access to the Countryside Act 1949 as amended by various other legislation, importantly the Countryside and Rights of Way Act 2000. These are outside the scope and purpose of this book.

The development of local authority libraries, museums and culture. is somewhat different to that for recreation. Whilst created by Acts of Parliament these early institutions were not part of the developing local authorities.

The history of public libraries commenced in the mid19th century and is based on the Victorian desire to improve the public, this time through education. The Public Libraries Act 1850 was the first Act. This was succeeded by other legislation, the latest being the Public Libraries and Museums Act 1964 which is still in force and set out the current duties for the provision of libraries by local authorities and power to provide museums.

Free museums and art galleries have been set up by Act of Parliament since the 18th century, such as the Act which created the British Museum and 19th century Act creating 'Albertopolis', the area in South Kensington London which created the Royal Albert Hall and museums. However, these created specific philanthropic and other trusts and are now run by charitable trusts. Local authorities are not responsible for these major national museums and art galleries.

Theatres have been commercial ventures in the UK for many centuries, for example the Globe and Theatre Royal Drury Lane in London. Local authorities do not own the majority of theatres.

Charitable and community ownership and management and community asset transfer

In addition to ownership of leisure centres, some theatres and cultural buildings and museums by local authorities there are a number of facilities (some smaller leisure centres, theatres, community centres or other) which are and have always been owned by local independent charitable trusts. These will have been funded and built out of donations not provided by the public sector. There are also a number of similar organisations which have been transferred from local authority ownership to a local community trust via an asset transfer on a long-term lease or even freehold. In some areas, these are an important local facility though they are not to be compared to the national organisations mentioned in the previous section.

They are mentioned here because whilst not examples of local authority owned services which are subject to procured relationships, they may be grant funded by a local authority or managed by a private sector contractor on behalf of the trust owner. They are part of an area's leisure and culture offering. These may or may not have a robust governance model for example because they do not have sufficient revenue to continue to maintain the buildings and provide services and/or they have difficulty achieving sufficient trustees.

Compulsory Competitive Tendering, its Implications and the Development of the Local Authority Leisure Trust

This section considers the impact of compulsory competitive tendering on the development of leisure procurement and the leisure trust.

The most important initiative which is relevant to this market was introduced by the Local Government Act 1988, was compulsory competitive tendering ("CCT"). Grounds maintenance including of parks and open spaces was included in the first wave of competition, leisure centres were part of a second wave requirement to be delivered by the end of 1992. Dual and joint use facilities, arts, culture and libraries were excluded.

CCT required local authorities to carry out an open market competitive process for in-scope services. A flourishing private sector grew up to bid for contracts for ground maintenance for parks and open spaces and to run leisure centres. These are the basis of the current private sector market.

Early contracts tended to be input based, prescriptive and designed to give the in-house services the best opportunity of 'winning'. Many local authorities did not support CCT and did not want to submit their services to competition.

Local authorities who did not support CCT looked at alternatives. One popular alternative was a local authority created philanthropic or wholly charitable trust. These models initiated the first wave of local authority led externalisation. These trusts could access non-domestic rate relief and could possibly be VAT efficient (See chapter 11.for taxation implications). The model was a transfer of leisure services by a specific local authority to a newly created local leisure trust with trustees from the local area including some local authority members, without any competition. The expectation was that savings would accrue because of more favourable taxation treatment for non-domestic rates and the trust would develop and grow. The precise services which were transferred would depend on the in-house services being delivered and the appetite for externalisation. The trust could be very small responsible for only one or two leisure centres or bigger with more centres plus a theatre or arts venue, sports development and other services with the first transfer of a wide range of services from the London Borough of Hounslow in 1998 (leisure centres, arts, museums, open spaces and libraries). Governance would either be an industrial and provident society (now a registered society) or a company limited by guarantee and charitable status might or might not be obtained initially. The trust would take a transfer of all local authority staff including the top management. Thereafter it delivered the ex-local authority leisure services via a single lease or a lease of each facility at a peppercorn, a funding agreement which could be called a grant agreement and possibly a contract for some services. The length of the lease(s) and agreement varied from 7 or so years with up to twenty years or even longer for the lease and potentially a funding or grant agreement notionally of the same length.

Whilst CCT was abolished in 1999 and replaced by best value via the

Local Government Act 1999, the multi-model marketplace was in existence by then consisting of private sector organisations who won CCT contracts and trusts. An increasing number of local authorities realised the benefits of a better value for money externalised model for the delivery of these primarily discretionary services, services which whilst not a statutory duty were and are very highly valued by the authority's community and are a core part of the government's health and wellbeing agenda.

Conclusion

The history demonstrates that local authority delivered or commissioned leisure and culture has a long and important history, a history which is still directly relevant to this day. The law which applies today is based on a line of legislation and cases, in some instances, going back to the nineteenth century.

It also assists in explaining the development of what is now a complex multi-model marketplace.

CHAPTER TWO

THE LAW – LEGAL BACKGROUND

In this chapter key legislation is briefly set out with an even briefer reference to any law which relates to leisure and culture though not part of the core focus of this book.

The following legislation will be considered:[1]

- Public Health Act 1936;

- Section.19 Local Government (Miscellaneous Provisions) Act 1976;

- Section 164 Public Health Act 1875 and Open Spaces Act 1906;

- relevant sections of the Local Government Act 1972 ("LGA 1972");

- Local Government (Contracts) Act 1997;

- Local Government Act 1999;

- Local Government Act 2000 still relevant for Welsh local authorities);

- Localism Act 2011(does not apply in Wales);

- Well-being of Future Generations (Wales) Act 2015 (does not apply in England);

- Public Services (Social Value) Act 2012 ((does not apply in

---

[1] Unless otherwise identified all legislation quoted applies in England and Wales.

Wales);

- Section 149 Equality Act (applies in Wales via a Welsh statutory Instrument);

- Public Libraries and Museums Act 1964;

Public Health Act 1936

As identified above, this provides local authorities with the power to provide pools in parallel with the Local Government (Miscellaneous Provisions) Act 1976.

Section 19 Local Government (Miscellaneous Provisions) Act 1976

Section 19 replaced earlier legislation and is the current general legislation which provides a local authority with specific power to provide sport and recreation facilities and activities within or outside its area (see section 19 (1)). Section 19 (1) defines recreational facilities very widely and includes indoor and outdoor recreation, sports centres, swimming pools, skating and all other sports. It specifically includes services ancillary to the core leisure provision, for example parking, food, drink and buildings, equipment and any supplies. Section 19(2) sets out the power for a local authority to make any facilities that it provides in pursuant of section 19 (1) available for use by such persons either without charge or on payment *"as the authority thinks fit"*. It is this subsection which provides for contracting with a third party for the delivery of leisure services. In my opinion this latter sub-section envisages that the local authority has to have an element of control over its pricing policies and those of third-party contractors, though there is no reason why this should not be light touch. It does not differentiate between different types of local authorities (see chapter 3)

This is a heavily litigated section and it has been held by the courts that it should be interpreted narrowly (*Credit Suisse -v- Allerdale District Council [1997] Q.B 306*). This case is one of a long line of cases which makes it clear that local authorities' functions can only be exercised specifically in accordance with the relevant statutory provisions. It is still good law although its importance is diminished in view of later legislation specifically such as the Local Government Act 2000 and the Localism Act 2011 (see below).

Local authorities can also provide financial support to voluntary organisations or another local authority by way of grant or loan 'towards the *expenses incurred or to be incurred* by that body in providing such facilities as the local authority may provide. to provide the opportunities (see section 19(3)). This is the historic section which allowed local authorities to grant aid the trusts which they set up (see chapters 1 and 5).

Like most of the cultural functions these are powers not duties.

LGA 1972

There are a number of sections of the LGA 1972 which are relevant. These are referred to in chronological order in this chapter.

Section 121 LGA allows principal authorities to purchase any land which they are authorised to purchase under any other legislation. Section 122 allows them to appropriate this from one purpose to another with some important restrictions in this and other legislation setting out steps such as advertisement of the disposal of land such as allotments or public open space or ring fencing the use of capital receipts.

Sections 123 – 130 LGA 1972 deal with land disposals. Section 123 (2) (a) provides that local authorities may dispose of any land as they think fit except that they may not dispose of land 'for consideration less than the best that can be reasonably obtained' except for a short tenancy of seven years or less unless there is an applicable general or specific consent under section 128. There are two relevant consents under section 128, *Circular 06/03: Local Government Act 1972 general disposal consent (England) 2003 disposal of land for less than the best consideration that can reasonably be obtained* and *Local Government Act 1972: general disposal consent (Wales) 2003 disposal of land by local authorities in Wales for less than best consideration*. These are similar and give general consent to disposals at less than best consideration without specific consent provided that the authority considers 'that the disposal would contribute to the promotion or improvement of the economic, social or environmental wellbeing of the whole or any part of its area, or all or any persons resident or present in its area' and the undervalue is for less than £2 million. The local authority should establish a proper purpose for the disposal and carry out a valuation to establish the true value of the proposed disposal. Disposal at an undervalue ought to be an exception as local authorities have fiduciary duties to their council tax payers. This is a common law duty owed by local authorities to their tax payers to act as trustees of public funds and enshrined in a number of cases (see *Roberts v Hopwood [1925] AC* 578). Disposal at an undervalue ought not to apply where this is pursuant to an open market procurement where a lease(s) is disposed of at a peppercorn as part of a suite of interconnected documents which together provide value (see chapters 9 and 11).

Section 123 (2A) for principal councils and section 127 for parishes and communities provides that open space land cannot be disposed of without an advertisement for two consecutive weeks in a local newspaper and consideration of any objections. In Wales, section 123 (2AA) provides that this does not apply if the provisions of the *Playing Fields (community involvement in disposal decisions) Wales measure 2010* apply. This measure provides for more extensive the advertisement and consultation than under section 123 (2A) in view of the importance of school playing fields in Wales.

The definition of public open space is as set out in planning legislation and may include land which has been built on as a leisure centre and not appropriated out of public open space land first (see sections 122 and 126 LGA 972). A disposal in breach of this legislation is arguably void and can be set aside certainly before completion but not afterwards (see sections 128 and 131 and *Structadene Ltd, R (on the application of) v Hackney London Borough Council* [2000] EWHC Admin 405). As it is not always clear whether or not land was acquired as public open space or is currently open space, prudence suggests advertising if there is any doubt. *Structadene* is just one of a large number of cases on disposal by local authorities.

It will be appreciated from the above brief description and analysis that the law relating to disposal of land may give rise to technical legal issues.

Therefore, whilst local authorities now have wide powers under the Localism Act 2011 (see below), it is always prudent to check the powers under which a local authority acquired and hold leisure land at an early stage to ensure that there are no impediments preventing a disposal or making this problematic either under local authority legislation or otherwise such as being charitable land or subject to restrictive covenants.

139 LGA 1972 provides power for local authorities to accept gifts of property. Historically much leisure land has been gifted to local authorities under this or predecessor legislation, often without an endowment. If there is an existing charitable trust, the local authority will take subject to this. The local authority becomes sole trustee but has no obligation to maintain the facilities under section 139 though may have general obligations if this is open space land. It may be necessary to apply to the charity commission for a scheme to reflect changing reality if there is no money to maintain a building and the local authority does not wish to do so, either because it is not fit for purpose or otherwise.

Section 144 LGA 1972 sets out powers for to encourage visitors for recreation and other purposes and as part of this provides powers to encourage others to provide or to provide conferences, trade fares or exhibitions and facilities for these. A number of local authorities manage or procure the management of these facilities as part of their leisure portfolio either as part of a suite of mixed buildings and activities or free standing and seek to externalise these are part of a leisure portfolio or otherwise.

Section 145 LGA 1972 empowers local authorities to do or arrange for the doing of anything or contribute to the to the expenses of doing anything if necessary or expedient in relation to an entertainment venue. This is a very wide power (c.f. section 19 above). Where an entertainment venue, for example a theatre or a mixed purpose entertainment space is externalised as part of an externalisation project this is not likely to cause similar technical issues to the leisure centre contract.

Public Health Act 1875 and Open Spaces Act 1906

Section 164 Public Health Act 1874 allows local authorities to purchase or lease any public walks or pleasure ground. The Open Spaces Act enables trustees of public open space land and others including charitable trustees to transfer this to a local authority and the local authority to accept the land (see sections 1 – 8). Local authorities acquired many of their leisure portfolio under this old legislation. Like acquisitions under section 139 LGA, much land was acquired under the Open Spaces Act without any or sufficient revenue endowment for its maintenance which is now a problem in view of local authority's financial constraints. In a number of instances, it was not clear whether the land was transferred under the Open Spaces Act subject to charitable trusts or not i.e. in a manner which allowed the local authority to manage and dispose of the land free of these or any other restrictions. Section 30 Charities Act 2011 will in most instances now require registration of land with the charity commission if that land was acquired and is held as charitable land. The local authority will be the sole trustee and have to manage the land subject to its charitable trusts. It is outside the scope of this book to set out the detailed provisions which apply when a local authority is a charitable trustee. They are enforced by the charity commission against all including local authorities and technically complex. Where a local authority is considering disposing of charitable land via a procurement (or otherwise) it is essential to consider the legal implications of this in detail at an early stage as it will be necessary to appoint separate advisors for the charity (see Charity Commission guidance, *Local authorities as charity trustees* and *Councillors' guide to a council's role as charity trustee*).

There are also a number of reported cases where there have been disputes over whether land owned by a local authority is held for charitable purposes (see *Bath and North East Somerset Council v Attorney General* [2002] EWHC 1623 (Ch)).

Section 10 Open Spaces Act provides that the land shall be held for the benefit of the public and shall be maintained 'in good and decent repair'. The extent and meaning of this are unclear but unlike section 19 Local Government (Miscellaneous Provisions) Act 1976, this is a statutory duty.

Local Government (Contracts) Act 1997

This clarified that local authorities may enter into contracts for the provision of their functions, something that prior to this was implied but not expressly stated (see section 1). The Act's purpose was to ensure that public finance initiatives ("PFI") were able to be completed by resolving uncertainty over power to enter into transactions. The private sector was unwilling to enter into these in view of the line of cases exampled by *Allerdale* (see above). The act also provides a process whereby contracts for at least five years for assets, services or both can be certified as within the powers of the local authority (intra vires) making it virtually impossible for such a contract to be challenged as outside its powers (ultra vires). Outside leisure PFI contracts the certification provisions are not generally used in this sector although it would be open to the private sector to seek a certificate.

Local Government Act 1999

This replaced compulsory competitive tendering by an obligation (i.e. a statutory duty) of best value, securing continuous improvement in the way its functions are delivered (section 1). A series of statutory instruments and guidance identified how this act was to be delivered. As part of these, cyclical processes of strategic service reviews and contracts which included performance standards and indicators were all becoming standard. These would demonstrate compliance with the principles and vision behind the Act and (in theory) enable continuous improvement to be demonstrated. All of this became standard practice and is still in place today. The act is still in force although the precise requirements for cyclical reviews and detailed requirements have been repealed as they were too onerous. In practice, the legislation in the next section has superseded it.

Local Government Act 2000, Localism Act 2011 and Well-being of Future Generations (Wales) Act 2015

The Local Government Act 2000 introduced the power to promote economic, social and environmental wellbeing with a requirement for local authorities to have a plan or strategy regarding delivery. In effect, this has been superseded by the general power of competence in the Localism Act 2011 in England and in Wales, the obligations under the Well-being of Future Generations (Wales) Act to improve the social, cultural, environmental and economic well-being of the people and communities of Wales. The spelling of wellbeing or well-being is different in English and Welsh law. For consistency, the English spelling is used throughout except when quoting legislation when the appropriate spelling is used. The various statutory provisions including the obligations on unitary authorities in England with health and social care duties to appoint a statutory director of public health to (see Public Health Act 2012) and the statutory obligations in Wales have all added to the blurring of the discretionary nature of leisure and recreation with the obligations on local authorities in England and Wales to consider and promote leisure insofar as it has health and wellbeing component.

One theme in recent legislation is to require joint working. These require the development of plans and initiatives in conjunction with other statutory bodies to improve the health and welfare of their residents and communities. These and the statutory interrelation between health, social care and leisure together with the public and government focus on increasing physical activity to reduce obesity, help mental and physical wellbeing and supporting greater activity including amongst school children all make it increasingly difficult to perceive leisure and recreation as purely discretionary and something which a local authority can choose not to provide. Without delivering, procuring or commissioning leisure provision, it is arguable that local authorities will fail to achieve their wider health duties and other expectations placed upon them as part of their public health responsibilities. They will find it very difficult to work with health bodies including GPS and others to achieve the government's requirements.

Legislation Applicable to Libraries and Museums

A detailed consideration of the duties and powers of local authorities in relation to libraries and museums is outside this book's terms of reference. However, as some leisure providers, also provide one or more of these services either as part of a leisure centre portfolio or otherwise, the legislation relating to these is mentioned in passing.

The Public Libraries and Museums Act 1964 provides that unitary authorities and county councils have a general duty '*to provide a comprehensive and efficient library service*' for residents and those who work in their area (section 7). This is a free service (section 8). Charging for service is limited to a small number and value of additional services such as copying or borrowing CDs.

The extent of the duty and what it means in practice with regard for example, to the number and geography of libraries in a particular local authority area is unclear. All local authorities will have a strategy and its annual implementation and whether there are any changes will form part of the annual service plan. The budget implications of this will be part of the local authority's budget planning and annual budget. If there are particular budget pressures which require the local authority to consider changes such as either closures or down grading a library from a full service to one provided by volunteers consultation may be needed and the plans may be challenged on the basis that to do so does not comply with the statutory service and/or there has been failure to carry out a proper equality impact assessment. Plans to close libraries or change the nature of the service is often highly contentious with a number of reported decisions arising from judicial review challenges (see for example one of the latest in a long line, *R (on the application of WX) v. Northamptonshire County Council and R (on the application of John Connolly) v. Northamptonshire County Council [2018] EWHC 2178 (Admin)*). Challenges are considered in more detail below (see chapter 6)

Unlike libraries, there is power rather than an obligation, to provide and maintain museums (section 12) and a power to charge admission for entry (section 13). In practice, most authorities do not charge for entry or charge a sum which does not cover the cost of running the museum. Local authorities also have the power to pay towards the expenses of others in maintaining their museum (section 14). Many municipal museums have been transferred to small trusts or closed in recent years.

Miscellaneous other Legislation

In addition to the above, there are a number of other acts which are particularly relevant to the content of any procurement, such as the evaluation matrix and the terms of the contract to be entered into between the local authority and contractor. These include the Public Services (Social Value) Act 2012 and the duties of local authorities under the *Equality Act 2010* and in particular s.149.

Public Services (Social Value) Act 2012 provides that a local authority in England should 'consider, at the pre-procurement stage, how procurement could improve the social, economic and environmental wellbeing of the relevant area, and also to consider how in conducting the commissioner might act with a view to securing that improvement. This means the local authority should think about the potential social benefit of a service from the start of the commissioning process.' (*Public Services (Social Value) Act 2012, An introductory guide for commissioners and policy makers*, DCMS 2012).

https://assets.publishing.service.gov.uk/government/uploads/system/uploads/attachment_data/file/690780/Commissioner_Guidance_V3.8.pdf). This is a statutory duty.

The *Equality Act 2010*, which is applicable in England and Wales, protects the rights of people who have protected characteristics. These include all of the characteristics of people who were protected under previous legislation and extends these. Key such characteristics are age, disability, gender reassignment, race, religion or belief, sex, sexual orientation, marriage and civil partnership and pregnancy and maternity. Local authorities have a specific duty to *'have due regard to the need to (a)eliminate discrimination, harassment, victimisation and any other conduct that is prohibited by or under this Act; (b) advance equality of opportunity between persons who share a relevant protected characteristic and persons who do not share it; (c)foster good relations between persons who share a relevant protected characteristic and persons who do not share it.'* (section

149). These protected characteristics and specific public sector equality duty are materially relevant to procurement for a leisure or culture service (see chapter 6).

Conclusion

The above is a very brief snapshot of the legislation applicable to the delivery of leisure and culture. The differing nature of the core legislation for the various services defies logic and can only be explained by history and a lack of consolidation. The more recent overlay of recent general legislation adds to the number of separate pieces of legislation that anyone considering a leisure centre contract need to consider.

———————————

CHAPTER THREE

WHICH TIERS OF LOCAL GOVERNMENT ARE RESPONSIBLE FOR DELIVERING AND/OR PROCURING LEISURE AND CULTURE?

Introduction

This chapter considers the allocation of indoor and outdoor leisure, arts, libraries and other relevant functions between the different tiers of local government. It also considers the overlap between the various tiers and what happens in practice.

Whilst this may be relatively clear in general, there is some overlap as some of the functions are concurrent.

It is outside the scope of this book to analyse the types of local authorities within England and Wales or the multitude of legislation changing its structure. However, it is necessary to identify the practical implications of the local government's structure on patterns of contracting and procurement for leisure and culture particularly as a number of functions are concurrent.

In brief, England is divided into one or two tier principal authorities i.e. either counties and districts or unitary authorities which may be metropolitan or include non-metropolitan areas as well because of re-organisation of two tier areas into single unitary tiers. In addition, some areas have parish or community councils. Wales is divided into unitary authorities and in some areas there are the equivalent of parish councils in England known as community councils or town councils.

Different tiers have primary responsibility for different services and it is this which is considered in outline below.

Indoor leisure and Sports Development

The functions under section 19 Local Government (Miscellaneous Provisions) Act 1976 are concurrent across all tiers. In practice, where there are two tier principal authorities, indoor leisure facilities are in general provided procured or grant funded by district councils. In single tier areas it is of course, the single tier authority who provides these. In some areas community/parish councils may provide or procure the provision of a leisure centre.

Dual or joint use facilities where there is a specific facility providing both community and school use have a more mixed pattern of delivery and funding and therefore procurement and contracting. Where there is a procurement this will usually be as part of the wider leisure procurement. Unless the community use is in a building which is wholly separate from the school use the dual nature of the provision will require the availability of community use to be part only of the weekdays during term time with wider holiday use.

The schools building programme in England (building schools for the future) has meant a number of new schools have been built with their own leisure facilities. The governing body chooses whether to provide any community access and if so, manage this in-house, or sometimes may seek to be part of their local authority's procurement.

To the extent that there is any sports development these will be delivered by a district or unitary and may or may not be retained in-house or externalised with the leisure centres. The delivery pattern is complicated because a number of county councils have set up county partnerships for sports development to deliver this in partnership with health and other bodies and may grant fund these

Parks and open spaces

There are concurrent functions, though in practice local parks are the responsibility of districts or unitary authorities. The grounds maintenance for the parks will also either be procured as part of the wider grounds maintenance functions or may possibly be part of the leisure centre contract though more usually it is only the activities in the park which form part of this.

County councils are responsible for national and county wide parks (see above).

Arts and culture

In practice, many theatres and other cultural institutions are delivered by independent trusts which may be part funded by local authorities. There are concurrent powers for all tiers, including parishes and town councils. Community arts and theatres would usually be part of a district or a unitary authority's general leisure and cultural offer and procured as part of a wider leisure centre offer.

Museums

In practice, many museums are delivered by small independent trusts which may be part funded by local authorities. There are concurrent powers for all tiers including parishes and town councils, though it is it districts or unitary authority's which provide or support the majority of these. As identified, community museums are not income generating and should be part of a district or unitary authority's general leisure and cultural offer and procured as part of a wider leisure centre offer.

Libraries

A library service is statutory and unlike leisure, arts and culture is the responsibility of a county council or a unitary authority, rather than a function of all tiers of local government. It is a specialist service with a very small private and voluntary sector delivery market for whole service transfer and a limited number of whole service externalisations. The position is different for library IT, books and other resources which are purchased through buying consortia. As this book is concerned with service transfer, this marketplace is outside the terms of reference.

Conclusion

Of the above services, only leisure centre and sports hall contracts could be said to be a flourishing multi-provider market. Theatres, museums and other cultural services are not secure income generators and are unlikely to add commercial value to a procurement.

CHAPTER FOUR

SOUND DECISION MAKING PROCESSES AND THE CIRCUMSTANCES WHERE CONSULTATION IS RECOMMENDED

Introduction

This chapter is about sound decision making in relation to leisure and cultural services, specifically, the implications of a challenged and how to avoid successful or indeed any threat of judicial review or other challenge such as a representation or complaint to the Department of Culture Media and Sport in relation to a library service.

As previously identified leisure is a non-statutory function. However, it is a local authority function which is highly valued by communities and there may be wider implications of any service changes for example because of the wider impact of leisure on health, and wellbeing and the impact on employment and the economy of a local authority area. Most local authorities will have a leisure and/or sports strategy for indoor and outdoor sports. This will identify all of the facilities and activities which are available locally (whoever provides them) and should analyse the extent to which these are sufficient for local needs based on national guidance. Leisure and its impact is likely to be referred to in some detail within economic regeneration and other policies as they are economic regenerators provided facilities are in the right position. All of these relevant policies would almost certainly have been widely consulted on before adoption. They will be publicly available and accessible. The implications of and impact on the strategy of any change will need consideration even if closure is because a facility is not fit for purpose or unaffordable if this reduces a local offering and/or may arguably have a disproportionate impact on people with protected characteristics. There are many reported challenges where these and other issues have been thoroughly explored.

Any changes to much loved facilities and services are likely to create a strong reaction. This can happen even if the outcome will be the replacement of an out-of-date facility with a new facility, though perhaps on a different site and with a notional reduction in capacity, where there is still sufficient local resource evaluated against national guidelines. Therefore, local authorities need to take particular care with the way that they explain and consult on any decisions which could or will make changes to their leisure portfolio. They should prepare for decisions in a pragmatic manner whether there is to be a consultation or not, anticipating that there may be a challenge accepting that the public may consider that they have a legitimate expectation to be consulted.

In view of all of the above issues and the likely sophistication of the public, being prepared for challenge is prudent. The primary objective is to ensure that anyone who seeks to challenge does not meet the judicial review test of having an arguable ground for proceedings. This initial test must be met before the High Court will give consent to issue proceedings. Whilst judicial review is notionally about the way that a decision is taken, this is arguably partly notional because in practice the courts also look at whether a decision is so irrational that it would not properly have been taken if there was proper consideration of all relevant matters and all irrelevant matters had been disregarded.

The importance of libraries as town centre and wider regenerators is also demonstrated as these add footfall to a town centre.

When is consultation prudent?

It is prudent to consider whether to consult if the outcome of change is to reduce the number of premises from which leisure is offered. It is not generally necessary to consult if there is simply to be a change in who provides the leisure services such as a replacement of an existing provider or an externalisation of an in-house service. However, the position may not be as simple as a change of provider.

The change in provider may be part of a transformation strategy and if so, it may be necessary to consult first on the strategy or major changes to it and thereafter on the detail of its implementation. A service transformation may include future closure on economic or other grounds possibly with development of additional facilities on an existing or different site. In those circumstances there may be a general impact on availability or accessibility of facilities and services, so a consultation is prudent or even required before the strategy is changed and, thereafter on the detailed implementation of this.

It will be seen from the above that the range of possibilities is extensive. Consideration of whether when consultation is needed will need detailed and careful consideration in each instance, will be fact sensitive and require the specific facts which are applicable to be considered against an analysis of the relevant case law, always taking a pragmatic approach. As identified in the next section, consultation is an expensive and time-consuming process and whilst a challenge is going through the courts it is unlikely that any decisions can be implemented. This is likely to create a practical problem. In most instances, the local authority will be required to take an early decision as an existing contract may be expiring shortly and there will be budget pressures. However, a challenge can take months or even years to complete so a balancing exercise is needed on whether it is better to consult or to proceed and hope that there is no challenge.

There is a recent Court of Appeal decision which is a good example of the implications of a challenge for a local authority. *R v. Caerphilly County Borough Council ex p. Williams [2020] EWCA Civ.296* demonstrates the lengthy timescale, scope of and extent of litigation which can ensue if there is a judicial review which meets the threshold for proceedings, even if the challenge is ultimately unsuccessful. The litigation was about the approval of a strategy for the provision of sports and recreation strategy for facilities for 2019 – 2029. It was triggered by anger about the proposed closure of a specific leisure centre in South Wales. The case was argued on the basis that the decision to adopt the strategy should have been taken by the Council not Cabinet, the Cabinet should have had regard to the cost of implementing the strategy and there was a failure to exercise of a duty to secure continuous improvement under the Welsh equivalent of section 3 Local Government Act 1999, the Local Government (Wales) Measure 2009. All of these arguments failed. During the course of the case there was a successful challenge to the closure of the leisure centre in 2019. In total, the cases took some two years to reach a conclusion.

There is even more extensive case law on proposals to close libraries and/or to replace local authority delivery of a library by a library staffed by volunteers. In these cases there is a more mixed outcome for local authorities as many more challenges have been successful. In *R. v Northamptonshire County Council ex p WX* and R. v *Northamptonshire County Council ex p John Connolly [2018] EWHC 2178 (Admin)* (heard together) even where a local authority was in the most dire financial position, a challenge against extensive closures of libraries can succeed if the outcome of a consultation process which has been carried out in a lawful and proper manner is not properly considered before a decision to make very significant service cuts.

Sound Consultation, an Overview

Sound consultation in general is outside the terms of reference for this book. It is referred to in outline and to explain the process of consultation for the in-scope services. There are broadly, two types of consultation, consultation on a strategy or change in provision in general and consultation which is carried out in contemplation of a procurement.

This sub-section considers the particular issues which are relevant to consultation on change of strategy or provision for leisure and culture and why these can prove so difficult in practice. Consultation which is carried out before or in contemplation of a procurement is considered in chapter 6.

As identified in chapter 2, leisure and culture are non-statutory services, though much loved (though libraries are a statutory service). There may arguably be limited or no justification for a local authority to spend significant sums maintaining or improving a leisure or cultural service at a time of massive pressure on local authority budgets because of COVID-19 and in general. Core statutory services may have to come first. Leisure is a capital hungry business, the fabric and facilities (such as fitness and other equipment) at leisure centres need regular refreshing and/or updating at regular intervals. The buildings may need replacing every generation or two. Without regular investment the services may not be able to continue. Buildings which were built in the 1970s and 1980s are now past their lifespan (see chapter 1).

COVID-19 has added to the pressure on general budgets and the cost of leisure and culture because of lock-down closures and the requirements of social distancing even when facilities can re-open. Some facilities may not be able to re-open fully or at all because of their design. All of this has a massive impact on longer term revenue streams. Theatres and other cultural activities and premises are suffering similar or even worse revenue problems and many of these may also not be able to open at all whilst there is a need for social distancing because of their layout. Whilst some of the issues for libraries are different, partly because they are statutory, these are services which are free to the public and the impact of social distancing and enhanced hygiene are equally problematic.

However, as identified closing buildings and/or reducing the extent of services in this sector brings its own difficulties and requirements to or expectations of consultation. There is no current easy answer now or in the future. Closure of some premises may be the only feasible though difficult way forward and it is possible that there will be more consultations on forced closures in future months and years.

The general principles relating to consultation must be followed namely, that it must take place when a decision is at a formative stage i.e. before any decision has been taken. The local authority must give sufficient reasons for any proposal to enable intelligent consideration and response, adequate time must be given for consideration and response and the outcome of the consultation must be conscientiously taken into account in finalising any proposals (see *R (Gunning) v Brent London Borough Council (1985) 84 LGR 168*, endorsed subsequently by the Supreme Court in *R (Moseley) v LB Haringey [2014] UKSC 56*).

The following is therefore extrapolated as general principles from the extensive case law and sector experience. The options and the rationale for the various options which are being consulted on or the single option if there is only one which is viable, should be fully identified and explained. Any reduction of options for consultation prior to this should be carried out in a rational and logical manner. All options do not need to be consulted on but if some are disregarded and not short listed for consultation, it is prudent to explain the reason for this.

The following is a snapshot of the matters which need consideration. They will vary depending on what is proposed. A comprehensive equality impact assessment (under the Equality Act 2010) is required and should be considered to assess the consequences for people with disabilities, older people or others with protected characteristics. Any specific consequences for other groups such as children should be understood and reflected in the consultation and decision-making reports. Ensuring consideration on the wider impact on accessibility because of transport routes, distance between facilities and impact on users who may not have cars as well as on car users is prudent. Where there is a net reduction in premises or other services an explanation of this and its economic impact is important even if the reality is that the local authority has to make substantial revenue budget cuts.

The reasons for closure of premises are some or all of the following; that they are is old, not suitable for current and future needs, disproportionately expensive to run with a significantly greater subsidy per user than other facilities in the local authority's portfolio or industry standards, there is limited parking for people with disabilities, it is on a limited site, it needs many millions spent on it to extend its life by a short time when the local authority has other pressing capital requirements and even if this is spent, it will still be revenue unaffordable. These are examples of factors which may be unpalatable but are the outcome of financial pressures and if the decision-making process and consultation are carried out properly should mean that any closure succeeds. It is not the function of the court to challenge a decision based on a rational analysis of a local authority's spending priorities. Even where there are members of the public whose minds may never be changed, giving them the opportunity to challenge the local authority and make representations is still important so that the local authority can demonstrate an open mind.

For a process to be robust, the public must have sufficient time and opportunity to challenge the local authority's position preferably in a series of open meetings (now of course on-line) as well as in writing. Thereafter all responses must be fully collated and analysed, preferably independently, so that they can be considered by the decision-makers within the local authority. It may be possible to make alternative savings either in the relevant departmental budget or elsewhere and the public's as well as officer and member suggestions should be considered properly even if rejected in the recommendations. Even where a decision is unpopular if it is taken on a proper basis it ought to be possible to approve it if made appropriately. The one exception to this is libraries where if there is insufficient availability to meet the statutory duty this may not be sound (see chapter 1).

A proper open consultation is likely to take a number of months, for example, six months or longer. This makes it essential to consider at an early stage in a decision process and well before the date when any procurement or re-procurement must be completed. It may be possible to shorten this process if budget pressures or the condition of the premises require this.

Conclusion

Sound decision making is fundamental to local authority processes and never more so than in this sector where decisions are often poured over by pressure groups who are seeking the grounds to challenge a local authority because they do not like the decision.

CHAPTER FIVE

SERVICE DELIVERY, THE CURRENT AND HISTORIC EXTERNALISATION OPTIONS

Introduction

This chapter describes the more common options, sub-sets of these and a number of less common options for the externalisation of leisure services. The focus is contracts for the delivery of a leisure service especially leisure centres though there is some consideration of the implications of including other community services e.g. a theatre, sports development or other community buildings and services. The majority of the content is equally applicable to the delivery of other cultural activities.

Most leisure contracts are primarily or wholly contracts for the delivery of the local authority's leisure centres and their services. Depending on the local authority, the contract may include activities in parks, some cultural and other services such as a museum a theatre and others. It is unlikely that a library service will now be included in a portfolio of leisure services, although this has happened in the past. Where it is provided by the local authority sports development may be included or may be retained in-house.

Where a portfolio of existing or older facilities is externalised, this is likely to include only limited capital investment by the contractor for specific aspects such as replacement of equipment and limited responsibility for repairs, maintenance and/or improvements. The reason for this is practical. Local authorities can borrow more cheaply than contractors and as the cost of borrowing increases the cost of services, it will be passed on potentially with a risk premium attached. It is not cost effective for this to be the responsibility of the contractor, the market's focus is service delivery not property maintenance (see chapters 8 and 9). The main exception to this is fitness equipment. Contractors may be able to buy or lease fitness equipment more cheaply than local authorities because of the size of their purchasing requirements and/or control of the type and re-fresh of these major income generators and repair of buildings where these are essential to the service delivery especially income drivers is prag-matic. Being reliant on local authority investment or repair schedules may not be commercially wise because of competing pressures on local authority budgets.

In each instance, the options are described below are described with brief implications from a practical (rather than academic) legal perspective. Only the main private and voluntary sector sub-options are identified.

Some options have a relatively transparent governance structure, others such as a PFI option, are complex because the structure reflects the com-mercial importance of taxation efficiency and risk allocation. There are some options, such as an externalisation with a lease and no supporting contract, which whilst they may not now nor ever have been common-place are important because of their long-term implications. They are identified because of the issues that they raise.

As identified in chapter 1, the externalisation of leisure centres is one of the longest and most well-developed of local authority markets, nearly 30 years of age. In addition to new and replacement procurement and other externalisations, there are a significant number of historic projects which are still delivering services, are based on an outmoded model and/or terms and where it is not always easy to be clear about the legal meaning or implications. These approaches raise practical implications and risks for local authorities, the service provider and advisors both during delivery and in any procurement.

This introduction sets the general scene and the options considered in detail are:

- in-house delivery (the comparator);

- an open market procurement leading to an outsourced services contract;

- a contract or funding agreement with an independent charita-ble/non profit distributing trust;

- an open market procurement leading to an outsourced services contract with a private sector hybrid structure;

- an open market procurement leading to an outsourced services contract with a consortium;

- LATCO/*Teckal* (local authority trading company/controlled company);

- a lease with no contract;

- DBOM – design build operate maintain;

- DBFO – design build fund operate;

- PFI (private finance initiative).

In-house delivery

In-house delivery is the baseline option. Prior to CCT (see chapter 1), most leisure services were delivered in-house. In this option, the services are delivered directly by a local authority and its staff or (rarely) more than one authority working together.

Staff are employed directly; the services and property are managed and in a similar manner to any other in-house services. All risks and benefits are retained by the local authority which has to pay the non-domestic rate) "NNDR") relief levied on each property. The value added tax ("VAT") treatment of income is now similar whether or not the services are delivered in-house or externally (see *London Borough of Ealing v Revenue and Customs Commissioners (Case C-633/15 [2017] BVC 35 ECJ)*) though because of their anomalous VAT position a local authority with an in-house service is more likely to exceed its partial exemption limit (see chapter 11).

There are still a significant number of local authorities in England and Wales which deliver some or all of their leisure including leisure centres and other provision in-house. There are also schools and colleges who deliver some in-house provision for the community though as they are more likely to be charities they may obtain NNDR relief.

The in-house option has no procurement implications.

When considering whether or not to externalise provision a local authority with in-house provision will evaluate the options against the benefits and disadvantages of their in-house option.

An open market procurement leading to an outsourced services contract

The procurement implications of this option and key contract conditions are considered in more detail in chapters 6 and 8. Therefore, the legal model is described in brief in this chapter.

The legal structure is an open market advertised procured solution, resulting a contract and premises leases between a local authority and a third-party contractor. Services, assets and people transfer. The procurement process will now need to be carried out in a transparent and fair process pursuant to the public procurement regime (see chapter 6). The appointed contractor will be the entity which is successful pursuant to the procurement process. The contract for a services contract is usually within a range of 7 – 15 years because of the need for the contractor to recover their investment. There may be some shorter or longer contracts, for example where there are specific circumstances. A shorter contract may arise because of concern about the local authority's ability to fund a discretionary service in the medium to long term and where it is considered that a contract with modifications is not appropriate. There may also be longer contracts for example, where there is contractor investment (see chapters 5 and 8).

The most common model which is the outcome of a procurement is a contract with a commercial contractor which has an associated charitable or non-profit-distributing ("NPDO") organisation. The NPDO can achieve NNDR benefits as part of the tendered structure. The commercial provider may be the contractor with the NPDO as sub-contractor or the NPDO may be the contractor with the commercial contractor as its sub-contractor. The NPDO may be a charity registered with the charity commission, an exempt charity registered with and regulated by the Financial Conduct Authority, accepted by Her Majesty's Revenue and Customs ("HMRC") as having charitable status or a NPDO with charitable and philanthropic objects without charitable status.

Alternatively, a true charity may bid either on its own or in partnership with another stronger charity who can provide investment and/or other commercial benefits or skills. In this example the bidding charity will have one of the governance models identified above but was not promoted by or associated with a commercial contractor.

Contract or funding agreement with an independent charitable/ non-profit distributing trust

There are two options which are included within this structure, an open market procurement as described in the previous model, where the charity or NPDO wins the contract via a competitive process (see above) or, a contract or funding agreement between a local authority and an independent NPDO (which may or may not become a charity) which the local authority has promoted and where the contract, associated leases or other agreement has not first been tendered.

The procured example is considered in the previous sub-section on open market procurements.

The non-procured example was increasingly the model of choice for many local authorities in the aftermath of CCT, during the later nineteen nineties onwards until changes to the public procurement regime in 2015/16. Before this the model was seen as an attractive alternative to CCT. Thereafter it was still a preferred model for local authorities who were attracted by the NNDR and VAT savings (see chapter 11) and because it would enable the parent local authority to have major influence in the governance of the NPDO via board membership and/or its power as the main or only third-party funder. It was perceived that the local authority would have a greater level of influence over a trust than an externally procured contractor. Before the private sector developed their

NNDR efficient models, they could not achieve NNDR benefits. The trade-off for a trust, a less robust operating model with limited real risk transfer and limited or no borrowing capacity was seen as acceptable. This was partly because it was envisaged that the NPDO would be able to expand and spread overheads becoming stronger over time. In fact in most instances, with some notable exceptions, the reverse has happened and successive local authority cuts in service and funding resulted in a smaller and weak operator. In the last few years, these early arrangements have been ending by effluxion of time. The weakness of the operator means that on a subsequent procurement the trust loses and hands over the services to a stronger commercial operator.

Changes to the public procurement regime by virtue of the two Directives, on procurement (*2014/25/EU*) ('procurement directive') and on the award of concession contracts (*2014/23/EU*) ('concession contracts directive') and subsequent public procurement regulations ("PCR") brought in by the United Kingdom government 2015 and 2016 (see chapter 6) ended the option of contracting with an independent NPDO (or indeed any other independent body) without an open market procurement where a contract is above the relevant threshold with one exception. It is still theoretically possible to enter into a grant funded arrangement with an independent third-party provider with associated leases as grants and leases are outside the PCR. However, as identified in chapters 4, 9 and 11 these have taxation and other disadvantages. Historically they could possibly have triggered State Aid breaches though as identified in chapter 12 the European State Aid rules have now been revoked.

In law, a grant is a gift and in view of the annual nature of the local authority council tax setting, if it is a true grant it will technically be an annual payment with no guarantee of a future payment. This gives the provider no business certainty. In addition, a grant is not a vatable supply and therefore as well as intrinsically uncertain it will be very taxation inefficient and thus not likely to provide value for money. The third problem with a grant has hitherto that of State Aid. It is currently unclear whether this will continue to be a problem for local authorities or third parties.

An open market procurement leading to an outsourced services contract with a private sector hybrid structure

In this model, the outcome of the procurement is a contract with a private sector contractor who sub-lets the services and facilities to a charity or NPDO which it has set up thus achieving NNDR relief. Each of the main private sector contractors have offer a slightly different model. Some of these models are longer established than others and in one instance there has been a model where there is a contract between the provider and local authority with the commercial contractor acting as agent.

Where there is a charity, it may be a company limited by guarantee (subject to charity commission registration) or may be a registered society (subject to FCA registration).

It is not appropriate to consider these models in any detail, there are differences between them and it is essential for the local authority which is procuring these services to include consideration of these models as part of any short listing process and to understand all of the implications including whether it will access NNDR relief.

An open market procurement leading to an outsourced services contract with a consortium

In this model, the outcome of the procurement is that a consortium of a leisure and non-leisure provider(s) bids. It is only relevant where there are extensive capital works funded by the contractor (see below under PFI).

Local authority trading company (LATCO), controlled or *Teckal* company

This model has become increasingly common in recent years once the option of promoting an independent NPDO was closed by the changes to the public procurement regime (see chapter 6).

The controlled company is sometimes known as a LATCO or *Teckal*. This is because of the European case which originated the legal principle that an entity formed by a contracting authority and controlled by them was treated as being part of the state (*Teckal Srl v Comune di Viano and Azienda Gas-Acqua Consorziale (AGAC) di Reggio Emilia Teckal* (C-107/98).

The procurement directive and concession contracts directive included this legal model for the first time, confirmed the criteria for it to apply and its legal consequences (regulation 12 in the public contracts regulations 2015 ("PCR") and regulation 17 in the concession contracts regulations 2016 ("CCR").

A description of the PCR and CCR is set out below (see chapter 6). The relevant regulations are similar, the only substantive differences related to the different nature of a contract under each of these regulations.

The regulations set out the basis on which a legal person is a body controlled by a contracting authority and therefore outside the PCR or CCR. A legal person is defined as not a natural person. This means that an award of a contract to such a legal person, which would otherwise trigger the need to comply with the PCR or CCR would not be a breach of the relevant regulations provided the legal person complies with all of the detailed technical requirements in the regulations.

Key requirements are that the contracting authority/local authority would have to exercise over the company a similar level of control as it would exercise over its own departments, more than 80% of its trading is carried out for the parent local authority and there is no direct private sector capital participation (regulations 12 (3) and (4) PCR and 17 (3) and (4) CCR). Regulations 12 (3) and 17 (3) specify in more detail what is meant by a control similar to that of its own departments. These say that '*it exercises a decisive influence over both strategic objectives and significant decisions of the controlled legal person*'. It is unclear what this means in practice (see below).

It is possible for a controlled entity or group to be set up and jointly controlled by several contracting authorities. Thus either more than one local authority can promote such a body or another local authority(ies) to join the group at a later stage enabling shared central and support services or skills to reduce overheads. In such circumstances, the control can be joint.

Funding to a controlled or *Teckal* company is considered funding to the state and was not classified as State Aid under European law so presumably will not be classified as the equivalent under whatever UK law replaces it although this is not clear.

The governance options for a controlled entity are similar to other governance options (see above) except that to obtain the NNDR benefits the governing document must be that of a NPDO and to obtain separate VAT treatment and potentially be able to have different terms and conditions and policies there must be sufficient separation.

The line between control as defined and freedom as needed to obtain the taxation benefits and enable any external skills to be obtained is unclear. There are unanswered questions for example, how far must the composition of the board be wholly representatives of the parent local authority, either members or officers together with other important unresolved issues in relation to the level of control versus day-to-day independence? By way of a more specific example, how far is it safe to include non-local authority elected members or employees on the board and what decision-making power may they have for example as chair with a casting vote? The body's decision-making powers must reflect the technical rules in the relevant regulations as the directives were expressed as codifying the previous case law. There is no case law on the new directives and the status of the extensive pre-directives UK and European case law is not altogether clear. If the local authority gets it wrong, the consequence is that the award of the contract will be an illegal direct award with all that follow from this.

The commercial implication of this model is limited risk transfer, limited or no borrowing capacity.

A lease with no separate contract

In some instances, local authorities lease their leisure centres and other facilities to a third party without there being any associated contract.

Where instead of a payment by the local authority to the contractor/lessee there is a payment by the provider/lessee a lease may be used with a rent paid by the provider/lessee to the local authority for use of the leisure centre. This could be a flat sum or a sum which may be partly based on a profit share or turnover.

There are also some historic arrangements where a long lease of 20 years plus has been granted with a service level agreement included as part of the lease and money is paid to the provider trust.

True leases with no associated contract are outside the public procurement regime.

There are a number of difficulties with these various options. A lease is far less flexible a model than a contract, changes must be made via a deed of variation whereas with a contract, variations can be made under hand enabling a simpler and cheaper process for changes to the specified services. In some circumstances, changes to a lease may need to be registered at HM Land Registry (see chapter 9). Leases are also subject to the constraints laid down by legislation and the courts via extensive historic case law, for example whilst a contract can be ended by notice, forfeiture is subject to court consent and even a 'keep open' clause requiring a leisure centre to be open to the public may well not be enforceable. Finally, the COVID-19 guidance under the public procurement regime is irrelevant (see chapter 9).

In conclusion, if the relationship is governed via a lease it is the law of property not public procurement law which governs it and whether the financial and other terms can be varied is a matter of property and general local government law.

Design build operate maintain ("DBOM") and design build fund operate ("DBFO")

Two main models with sub-groups are described in this section.

The first is where the contractor will design, build and operate a new leisure centre either as part of a wider contract to operate a portfolio or for a single free-standing new facility. In this model, the local authority will provide the capital funding out of their reserves, prudential borrowing, third party grant or a combination of all of these. This model requires the contractor to be appointed prior to the design of the proposed leisure centre so that it is the contractor who designs the facility and manages the building programme. It is possible for the local authority to continue to manage the existing facilities and services or for these to be transferred to the contractor prior to the commencement of the building programme.

The second model is where the private sector will also fund a new facility and provide extensive capital rather than the more limited funding provided under all of the previous models which have been identified. This model has many similar characteristics to a PFI.

There are also examples of revenue contracts where a transformation programme is envisaged and is to be planned and delivered by the contractor as part of the contract. This is a model with some characteristics of a revenue contract and some of a DBOM.

Each of these models require a more sophisticated and detailed planning and procurement process together with legal documents than a conventional services contract (see chapters 5 and 6) and will therefore be more expensive, complicated and lengthy to deliver. In addition, where capital funding is required from the private sector, there are only a small number of leisure contractors who are able and willing to provide this. The majority of contractors do not have the funds and do not want to borrow. They do not need to get involved in such risky and expensive transactions as there are enough conventional revenue contracts available in the market. Historically, this has been a market with a significant number of opportunities for leisure contractors and the bigger contractors have been able to pick and choose which to bid for.

Private finance initiative ("PFI")

There are a small number of leisure centre PFIs especially in England where the PFI contractor has designed, built, funded and operates a facility via a PFI process and contract without it being part of a wider PFI.

There are also a number of PFI leisure facilities which have been built as part of a wider PFI, for example school PFIs as part of the building schools for the future programme in England where the leisure centre is part of this programme as a dual use community leisure centre or even where the PFI is part of a wider redevelopment. The leisure centre may be built using planning money. The PFI contractor will not tend to have any leisure specific experience and the leisure centre may be seen as a future management problem within the larger PFI contract. The leisure contractor could be procured by the PFI contractor or may be procured separately by the local authority as part of a wider leisure contract.

PFI contracts are between twenty-five years and up to thirty-five years long so within that period there may be several leisure contractors. The school and/or PFI provider authority may seek assistance from the relevant local authority in managing the process of securing a leisure centre contractor. There are many different variations within the PFI market and whilst it is not likely there will be any more true PFIs in the near future, or at all, these contracts, mostly entered into under the public contracts regulations 2006 still have many years before they end.

This is a valid marketplace model which needs to be included in any description of governance and management models, though is not common compared to the overall number of leisure contracts.

Conclusion

The above snapshot demonstrates the varied nature of this marketplace with sub-examples of the main examples and therefore the difficulty for practitioners who may be asked to interpret a set of arrangements many years after it was entered into and once all who were involved originally have left the local authority.

It is not always possible to interpret historic models, the meaning of the legal documents and/or how the relationship can be ended.

CHAPTER SIX

PUBLIC PROCUREMENT REGIME AND PROCUREMENT PROCESS

Introduction

In this chapter the following will be considered:

- an outline of the history of procurement of leisure and culture prior to the PCR and CCR. This includes its relevance today by reference to the current regulations;

- definitions and characteristics of a public contract and a concession contract;

- where the PCR is relevant, sound approaches to procurement and processes for leisure and culture;

- where the CCR is relevant, sound approaches to procurement and processes for leisure and culture;

- government guidance on COVID-19 and its legal impact. This will include consideration of the guidance within the procurement policy notes ('PPN'), published by the Crown Commercial Service, use of urgency procedures and modifications (variations);

- some general, practical and policy issues before you start

This chapter considers how the public procurement regime applies specifically to leisure and culture contracts. These are specialist contracts and the chapter does not seek to set out a full exposition or analysis of the regime.

For the purposes of this chapter, the contracts are presumed to be either wholly services contracts or contracts where the vast majority of the value is the services element and it cannot be argued that this is a works contract. Even where a contract includes some elements which are not services such as works and/or supplies, these are likely to be far less than the total contract value, even where a contract is a PFI. There may possibly be a very small number of contracts which are building contracts and where the services element is less than the total value, this is unlikely and will require specialist advice.

There is available marketplace guidance on the leisure and cultural technical aspects of procuring a leisure and cultural service from Sport England and the specialist leisure consultants who advise on these sectors. The focus in this section is therefore the more specific and technical legal aspects. As the application of the PCR is still relatively new law and there is limited case law there are a number of legal aspects and issues which are unresolved and may well remain unresolved for many years. Whilst local authorities quite properly seek practical approaches to procurements which are acceptable to the market an understanding of the legal complexities may be needed.

Finally, in this chapter there is consideration of some of the general, practical and policy issues which ought to be looked at before any procurement is started.

An outline of the history of procurement of leisure and culture prior to the PCR and CCR

As identified above, full coverage of above threshold procurement under regulations was only introduced into UK law because of the directives on procurement (*2014/25/EU*) ('procurement directive') and on the award of concession contracts (*2014/23/EU*) ('concession contracts directive') and subsequent public procurement regulations ("PCR") brought in by the United Kingdom government ins 2015 and 2016. There was no directive governing concessions before 2014 and they were governed exclusively by articles in what is now the Treaty on the Functioning of European Union ('TFEU') which were only relevant if there was a European market. There was no European market for leisure, culture and libraries.

Leisure, culture (including libraries), arts and other services were originally considered anomalous or 'Part B' services under the public contracts regulations 2006, the predecessor regulations to the PCR. They were not included in the list at Part A of Schedule 3 of these regulations. Services included in the list at Part A required full compliance with these regulations. Services not included were not. The consequence of the Part B status meant that only very limited parts of these regulations were applicable.

There will be many existing leisure contracts which were procured under the public contracts regulations 2006. This will be relevant when considering variations or modifications to these contracts (see below).

Although, historically, leisure, theatre and arts procurements were considered Part B services under the public contracts regulations 2006, in 2011/12 understanding of the law changed because a recent European court case was followed in the Court of Appeal. This confirmed that the definition of a concession was wider than had been thought. The case, *JBW Group Limited v Ministry of Justice [2012] EWCA Civ 8* is about a bailiff's contract for execution of warrants, where even though all money was paid by third parties to the bailiffs and there was no guarantee of any particular level of work as the numbers of warrants issued would depend upon a varying number of defaulters, this was a concession. It was accepted that by both parties that the contract was a concession in the recently reported decision, *Westminster City Council v Sports and Leisure Management Ltd [2021 EWC 98 (TCC).*

Once leisure and culture contracts were understood as likely to be concessions the legal considerations changed. Prior to the 2014 directive there was no directive which applied to concessions. Therefore, there was a strategic issue for consideration, the extent to which European law applied and whether it applied at all. As local authorities are required by their own internal constitutions and in particular contract standing orders and financial regulations, to advertise large contracts via an open competition, numerous procurements, which for many local authorities included advertising in OJEU, demonstrating whether there was any European interest for leisure and culture contracts and engagement of TFEU issues was relatively simple. Numerous openly advertised procurements identified that there was no European market for these services because no European companies had bid. As there was no European market the better view was that the TFEU was not engaged and if it was a concession contract, a leisure or culture contract was governed solely by UK law. This is still the position.

Whether libraries and possibly museums were concession contracts required separate consideration because neither of these services provide a similar pattern of income risk as there is little or no income for the core services and activities. The position was certainly potentially different for Library procurements. They may properly have been Part B procurements prior to 2015. This was possibly the position for museum procurements, although this is less clear.

However, where various services were procured together it was less clear what they were and this may well have depended on which contractual element was larger.

The history is important because the majority of leisure and cultural contracts are and will be for a relatively long period. Contracts for less than 10 years are unusual. Thus of existing contracts, most will have been let under the previous procurement regime. This will probably be the position for some years to come. As the public contracts regulations 2006 did not apply and there were no regulations applying to concession contracts there are some contracts which were not even let following an open market procurement. This has commercial and legal implications (see below).

The Current Law, Definitions and Characteristics of a Public Contract and a Concession Contract

This section considers the definition of a public contract within the PCR, the definition of a concession contract within the CCR and the implications. As identified above, the base line law is set out in the relevant directives. These were brought into UK law by the PCR or the CCR as applicable.

This book is a practical guide, the UK has now left the EU and there have been limited changes to the regulations to reflect this as set out in *The Public Procurement (Amendment etc.) (EU Exit) Regulations 2020, SI*

1319 ('2020 regulations') the focus in this section is on what the regulations say rather than the directives although there is consideration of the relevant directive, where appropriate. In addition, because the regulations follow the directives to a very significant extent the regulations will be sufficiently detailed for the practitioner.

The PCR and CCR have been amended from 1st January 2021 by the above 2020 regulations. These are said to be interim and connect with the Trade Bill currently going through Parliament, which will not be ready before the 31st December 2020. These are regulations intended to fix deficiencies in retained law and *'to preserve in these Regulations the duties owed, and remedies currently afforded to trade partners of the World Trade Organisation Agreement on Government Procurement for a period of 12 months'* (Government's comments in laying these before Parliament). These changes are technical changes and do not attempt to change the substantive law except to the extent necessary to reflect the UK's changed status outside the EU. There are likely to be further changes as the UK's trading position with the world becomes clearer and it is possible that the Government will realise that there is no merit in continuing to follow the EU directives and approach to procurement. If so, the UK could either revert to its historic common law position or adopt something wholly different. The Government is currently consulting and issued a *Green Paper: Transforming public procurement* on 15th December. As the consultation period does not finish until 10th March 2021 and thereafter there will need to be consideration of the responses and then legislation it is unclear when there will be more substantial changes. The timetable for this is not set out in the Green Paper. The 2020 regulations are a difficult read. Part 1 sets out general changes, Part 2 amends and repeal the primary legislation, Part 3, sets out changes to secondary public legislation (PCR and CCR), Part 4 amends the retained EU legislation and Part 5 amends international agreements. Most of these are technical amendments arising from leaving the EU and in due course, the changes will be made to the printed versions of the relevant legislation.

Where a procurement starts prior to 31st December 2020 the 2020 regulations confirms that the current regime will apply. The implications of this are unclear because there may be changes which are required because of the UK's status after the transition period has ended, for example publication of notices.

On 10th December, a policy note was issued together with frequently asked questions:

Procurement Policy Note –Public Procurement after the Transition Period ends on 31 December 2020, Information Note PPN10/20https://assets.publishing.service.gov.uk/government/uploads/system /uploads/attachment_data/file/943006/PPN-1020-Public-Procurement-After-the-Transition-Period.pdf

Annex A, Frequently asked Questions: End of Transition Period (TP)December 2020 https://assets.publishing.service.gov.uk/government/up-loads/system/uploads/attachment_data/file/943007/FAQ-for-PPN-1020-Public-Procurement-After-the-Transition-Period.pdf

These are short and identify the new process for advertisements from now until any further changes in the law.

Although Part B has been abolished there are specific provisions in the PCR and CCR for leisure, culture (libraries, arts and museums) services together with other services such as social care. These procurements are what is known colloquially as 'light touch' services because they fall within CPV (common procurement vocabulary) codes 92000000-1 range. 'Light touch' means that not all of the relevant regulations apply because it was considered by Europe that there is no Europe wide market for these services. Unlike the Part B or residual classification in the public contracts regulations 2006, the 'light touch' classification applies only to the specified CPV categories set out in the relevant schedule to the PCR or CCR. Any CPV not mentioned is subject to the full rigour of the regime. There is no change to that regime under the 2020 regulations. The CPV is a single classification system developed by the EU to stand-ardise the description of contract types. After 31st December 2020 changes to the CPV will be amended by the Cabinet Office Minister by statutory instrument (see the 2020 regulations).

The expression 'light touch' is not used in either the PCR or CCR though the expression 'light regime' is used in the directive. The expression 'light touch' is used very widely including in the guidance issued by the Crown Commercial government guidance, *The public contracts regulations 2015 & the utilities contracts regulations 2016, Guidance on the new light touch regime for health, social, education and certain other service (updated October 2016)* and see

(https://assets.publishing.service.gov.uk/government/uploads/system/uploads/attachment_data/file/560272/Guidance_on_Light_Touch_Regime_-_Oct_16.pdf).

Although there is Crown Commercial Service ('CCS') guidance on concession contracts, *Handbook for the Concession Contracts Regulations 2016*, there is no separate guidance for 'light touch'. paragraph 11.1 of the guidance says that '*The general contents of CCS guidance on the Light Touch Regime is also relevant for concession contracts for social and other specific services. In particular, concession contracts placed under the LTR [sic]are to be subject to the standstill period.*'

(https://assets.publishing.service.gov.uk/government/uploads/system/uploads/attachment_data/file/528062/20160607_Handbook_for_the_Concession_Contracts_Regulations_2016_final.pdf).

The current thresholds for '*light touch*' procurement is, for '*light touch*' public contracts, £663,540" and for all concessions £4,733,252. These will continue until first change on 1st January 2022. Thereafter, under the current law, these will change every two years using the same criteria as currently. The decision on the changes will be made by statutory instrument on the recommendation of changes the Cabinet Office Minister (see the 2020 regulations). It is this minister who is responsible for changes to the PCR and CCR after 31st December 2020.

The Green Paper referred to above is consulting on the abolition of the 'light touch' regime to replace it with the proposed simplified single system for procurement. The full coverage by the 2014 directives and as a consequence by the PCR and CCR means that with some specific public law exceptions (such as controlled or *Teckal* companies or administrative arrangements known as the *Hamburg* exemption after the EU case (*Case C-796/18 ISE v Stadt Köln (1)*) there are no above threshold procurements which are outside the rigour of the public procurement regime.

Deciding which set of regulations apply will require consideration of the expressed purpose or objectives of the procurement and its key terms including an analysis of the proposed terms on which the local authority is intending to procure. The outcome of what is in practice a comparative analysis may be obvious or may be less so in the current COVID-19. Culture in all its forms including recreation have been amongst the hardest hit of all services and it is envisaged future procurement may be significantly affected with terms offered by the marketplace being markedly different. An important relevant consideration may be the service mix and whether the procurement is for a relatively coherent group of services such as a leisure centre or several centres or a more mixed service portfolio including parks and open spaces, theatres, museums and culture or even a portfolio of services which includes libraries (though this latter is very unusual). The classification of the service portfolio which is greater in value will govern the issue of which set of rules apply.

By way of further clarification, a contract which supports a leisure or cultural service but is not itself such a service, for example a contract for IT services is not classified as 'light touch' even though it is for a social service.

The PCR 2015 identifies its purpose in regulation 3 in rather convoluted language. This says it sets out the procedure rules for procurements for pecuniary interest by contracting authorities for public contracts which are estimated to be not less in value than the relevant threshold and not otherwise excluded from compliance by the regulations. This means in plain English that where a contracting authority, in this instance a local authority, estimates that the likely tendered price for the contract is at or above the threshold and the contract falls within the definition of a public contract within the PCR, the local authority must carry out a PCR compliant process.

Whilst the PCR does not expressly define value as the sum or sums paid by the local authority or third parties to the contractor and by third parties this is implicit in regulation 6(1) which says that '*the calculation of the estimated value of a procurement shall be based on the total amount payable, net of VAT, as estimated by the contracting authority, including any form of option and any renewals of the contracts as explicitly set out in the procurement documents*'. Articles 29 and 30 to the preamble to the Public Procurement Directive 2014, identify that the definition of a public contract in regulation 2 is a contract for pecuniary interest as does the information required in the OJEU notice set out in paragraph 7 of the relevant Annexes to the directive. This latter identifies the information required in notices.

A recent European decision (*Case C 367/19 Tax-Fin-Lex d.o.o. v Ministrstvo za notranje zadeve*) has also clarified the position stating that where there is no consideration the procurement cannot fall within the definition of a public contract. In this case the offer was to provide the services for nil consideration. The logical implication of this is that even if a proper calculation is carried out prior to the procurement under regulations 3 and 6 that the estimated payment or value to the contractor for the contract is an above threshold payment and the values come in below the threshold it cannot be subject to the requirements to procure under the PCR. This issue will require further case law to clarify whether this interpretation is indeed correct or not. At present, the position is unclear.

No contractor will deliver a contract of this nature and complexity for minimal or no consideration without obtaining a financial reward. If the contract or management fee is nil the logical conclusion is that the recompense will be received elsewhere, for example from income generation. This raises a concern and risk that on a proper analysis of procurement law the contract was always a concession and the wrong process was followed.

A contract which is not a public contract under the PCR may be a concession contract or a utility contract. Utility contracts are outside the scope of this book. The exclusions from the PCR are set out in sub-section 3 to the PCR, regulations 7 – 12.

The CCR 2016 sets out the definition of and procedure rules for concession contracts. A concession contract is also defined as a contract for pecuniary value. However, the definition of pecuniary value for a services concession is the estimated total turnover of the contractor (referred to as the concessionaire within the CCR) generated from the contract (referred to as the concession) during the contract period as estimated by the contracting authority (regulation 9).

A concession contract is a contract where services are managed by the contractor where either the consideration is wholly in the right to exploit the services i.e. for no payment or is this together with a payment. There must be a transfer to the concessionaire of operating risk which involves *'real exposure to the market'* and where the concessionaire is not guaranteed to recoup the investment or costs incurred in delivering the contract (article 5 (1) directive and regulation 3). This does not mean all risks are transferred just sufficient for the contract to fall within the CCR. Transfer of risk of income from users is an example of the usual risk transfer in this sector. Applying the above to leisure contracts, the underlying assumption is that the income depends to an extent upon the competence of the contractor and income is a risk that the contractor is best able to manage. Of course, income also depends on many other factors such as the nature of the portfolio, its size, catchment area, the extent of any competition and last but not least whether the leisure facility is able to be open in full and in part. Even where leisure and other facilities can fully re-open post COVID-19 it is unclear how far users will be willing to come through the door and how quickly income will recover. COVID-19 therefore creates a specific set of factors and problems. The post COVID-19 position is currently very unclear as the impact of the pandemic is still current and continuing.

Income risk will usually be only one of the risks being transferred because certain or all repairing obligations pursuant to leases will also be transferred (see chapter 6). Property responsibilities are also likely to remain pursuant to the terms of the procurement even if the facilities centre cannot be opened or fully opened as the buildings will need to be maintained and repaired.

Whether there is *'real exposure'* as required by the CCR will be a question of fact. It is likely that the risk transfer will be partial. The contractual implication of a change of law provision whereby if some income risk remains with the local authority, for example where there is a change of law which requires full or partial closure of facilities is dealt with in chapter 6.

As identified, the position for libraries and potentially museums is likely to be different. As identified in (see chapter 2) the majority of library services are free and they therefore have very limited income. However, some libraries may be part of a multi-activity cultural facility including a leisure centre and/or conference centre. The opportunity for a real operational exposure or risk transfer is limited if a stand-alone library service is being contracted out though may be significant for a wider portfolio. Similarly, most museums provide their core services free, though there may be special exhibitions and an income from a shop. In practice as museums are commercially unattractive and local authorities tend to retain only one or a limited number of museums it is unlikely that a museum service will be externalised on its own. If a library and a museum service is externalised as part of a mixed procurement which includes other cultural services such as a conference centre, leisure centres and/or theatres the legal regime that applies is established by considering regulation 4 PCR and regulation 20 of the CCR. As identified the outcome of this consideration will be fact specific.

The directive and CCR are identical in the words used to describe '*payment*' though there is no precise definition of the word in either set of regulations. '*Value*' is defined in regulation 5 of the PCR by reference to the threshold and in detail in regulation 9 of the CCR. In the CCR can include a payment from or to the local authority i.e. an either way payment (see regulation 9 (7)) whereby the contractor receives a payment in part from the local authority and part via user payments which are uncertain.

Prior to COVID-19 it was not uncommon for leisure centre contracts to include a payment from the contractor (concessionaire) to the local authority for some or all of the contract period. This, together with a peppercorn lease(s) on a split repairing basis or where the contractor takes most repair risk would be part of the suite of documents (see chapter 9). It is unclear how far post COVID-19 modifications/variations and new post COVID-19 contracts will mean that this historic commercial basis for contracting will materially change and the extent to which new contracts will be concessions or PCR contracts (see the next section). Similarly, whether the market will ultimately recover, if so when and any wider implications of the pandemic on commissioning and procurement models are also unclear and are likely to remain unclear for some time.

It is usual for all of the financial provisions will to be in the contract, rather than split between the leases as this is more tax efficient for the local authority (see chapter 6).

The current thresholds are substantially different depending upon whether the PCR or CCR applies. Prior to 31st December the threshold in Euros and UK pounds for a PCR contract was 750,000 Euros and £663,540 respectively. The figure for the PCR reflects the fact this is a 'light touch' contract (see below). The threshold is the same for all types of concession contracts. Prior to 31st December was 5,3500 Euros and £4,733,252 for concessions. The government has said in the 2020 regulations that the thresholds are translated into pound sterling and the Euro comparator disappears. As identified above, the same thresholds will remain in place until 31st December 2021 and thereafter responsibility for their increase will be with the Cabinet Office Minister. The 2020 regulations also state that thresholds will increase on a similar basis to the basis when the UK was in the EU.

The implications of advertising under the wrong legal basis prior to 2015 was arguably not particularly material unless there was a challenge because the only practical implication would have been that the local authorities followed an unnecessary process. Whilst there were a number of threats of procurement challenge none progressed to court proceedings.

The position is now different as every above threshold procurement is covered by one of the PCR and CCR. Now there is full coverage the implications of following the wrong process could be very significant indeed. There have been a number of challenges and therefore a line of cases on the implications of not following the public procurement regime, letting a contract or disposing of land in breach. These include the line of cases which applied a wide interpretation to the definition of a works contract to a contract. In *La Scala (Ordine degli Architetti (La Scala) (Case C399/98) [2001] E.C.R. I-5409)* a development agreement thought to be a land transaction and thus outside the PCR was held to be a works contract which should have been procured under the then Italian equivalent of the PCR and this was followed in the later case of *Auroux (Auroux v Commune de Roanne (Case C220/05) [2007] All E.R. (EC) 918)*. *Auroux* was also about a development, in this instance a complex leisure centre development. There is a line of more recent UK cases regarding the definition of a concession for developments thought to be land transactions. This includes a recent court of appeal case regarding the scope of the CCR in relation to transactions which were arguably land transactions, *Ocean (Ocean Outdoor v London Borough of*

Hammersmith & Fulham [2019] EWCA Civ 1642). In this instance, the court of appeal held that the lease of land for advertising screens was a lease and not a concession contract. The case also considered damages for breach.

Whilst there may be no case law on the implications of following the PCR when the procurement should have been under the CCR or vice versa it follows logically that the implications could be similar to treating a works contract or concession as a land transaction and not carrying out a procurement. A failure to challenge using the remedies procedures under the regulations that were used or the correct regulations is arguably irrelevant because the procurement is bad from the beginning (see *Auroux*), the remedies cannot apply in such circumstances and are irrelevant (see below for consideration of remedies). This view is put forward on the basis that it is an unresolved legal area. It is accepted that the view may be controversial. If this view is correct it highlights the importance of lawyers and procurement officers analysing the nature of their proposed procurement and following the correct procedure.

As identified, the issue may become more important post COVID-19 because it may become less clear which procedure is correct. The extent to which the market agrees to accept income risk and this and other risks can be transferred may diminish significantly especially if a contract is a short-term contract using urgency procedure under the PCR because of existing contractor failure (see below). In future procurements and contracts, there may be little or no risk transfer for short term or even longer contracts.

The practical procurement and post procurement contractual implications of whether a contract is a 'light touch' PCR or CCR contract have differences are different so they are dealt with below in the relevant section.

It should be noted that public procurement is theoretically devolved to the Welsh, Scottish and Northern Ireland Governments. However, the Government has said it will retain this function centrally after December 31st 2020. It is unclear when it will be devolved once more.

To conclude on this section, the law is technically complex. The sheer number of European and UK cases demonstrates the difficulty in establishing whether or not the public procurement regime applies and if so, which set of regulations apply. The position may become less clear for leisure and cultural procurements in the future because of the impact of COVID-19 on patterns of procurement. The outcome of this is that each proposed procurement may need to be considered with care to establish its legal nature before the procurement is commenced.

Sound Approaches to Procurement and Processes for Leisure and Culture Where the PCR is relevant

Introduction

This section sets out an outline of the key issues and processes which apply if a procurement is undertaken pursuant to the PCR. The procurement implications of their application is analysed in outline focussing on the service specific legal issues for leisure and culture. Whether or not the PCR applies was considered in outline in the previous section.

The Approach and Process

Chapter 3 PCR, headed Particular Procurement Regimes, with a subheading Social and Other specific Services sets out the regulatory regime for the award of 'light touch' services and other things. Regulation 74 says it applies to the award procedure. By inference it does not exclude other provisions of the PCR from the rigour of the PCR. Only Regulation s 74 and 75 are relevant to this section.

Chapter 4 deals with strategic consultation. This section considers pre-procurement consultation.

Regulations 40 and 41 set out the provisions for preliminary market consultation before a procurement commences is not a requirement for 'light touch'. It does contain useful guidance and sets out a number of sensible suggestions. Regulation 40 says that local authorities may carry out market consultation with a view to preparing the procurement and informing the market of their plans. Seeking or accepting advice from independent experts or others or market participation is allowed although there is an overarching requirement in regulation 41 that the contracting authority should take appropriate measures to ensure that competition is not distorted by such participation. This is a very competitive market and contractors may have a number of bidding opportunities so it is sensible to ensure that there is sufficient interest for the forthcoming opportunity by for example publicising this and the likely terms to establish market interest or simply notifying contractors and trade associations that the opportunity to bid will occur in the near future. This consultation may well be carried out by leisure consultants appointed to assist the local authority.

A full public consultation is not commonplace before a procurement as this is likely to have been carried out as part of the consultation on policy referred to in chapter 4. An exception to this is where a service transformation, re-configuration of facilities and possible closure is envisaged as part of the proposed contract. In those circumstances it may be sensible to carry out a more extensive consultation before a procurement commences to avoid the risk of entering into commercial commitments, then carrying out a consultation and thereafter changing the terms of an existing contract after a later procurement. This may not be achievable as it will depend on the contract terms or if achievable may give rise to compensation and thus unaffordable leaving the local authority stuck between a contractual and service rock and a hard place.

For an above threshold 'light touch' process, regulation 75 says that there is a requirement to advertise the opportunity in accordance with Part H to Annex V to the Public Contracts Directive or if a prior information notice process ('PIN') is adopted in accordance with Part I to Annex V to the Public Contracts Directive. This is not substantially different to the information required for non-light touch procurements as the European principles of transparency and equal treatment apply. The new UK e-notification service called Find a Tender (FTS) now applies (see 2020 regulations and Cabinet office guidance, *Public-sector procurement from 1 January 2021*

https://www.gov.uk/guidance/public-sector-procurement-from-1-january-2021.

The information to be included in these notices is substantively unchanged. Contract notices require the name and address of the authority(ies)', the place of service delivery, a brief description of the proposed contract including CPV codes, conditions and time limit(s) for participation and the brief description of the main features of the award procedure to be applied. In the case of a PIN the information also includes the estimated total value of the contract, and duration of the contract and time limits for receipt of expressions of interest. The level and extent of the required information is a reflection of the European requirements *'to ensure compliance with the principles of transparency and equal treatment of'* contractors (see regulation 76 (2)). These requirements limit the changes that can be made during the procurement process. In practice, a sensible local authority will include considerably more information including a full description of the facilities and services required order to encourage interest both at the advertisement stage and later stages of the procurement.

There are no specific requirements in the PCR between the advertisement and the post award notification to OJEU (see regulation 75) for *'light touch'*. Like the contract notice and PIN, the award notice for a *'light touch'* is similar to the non *'light touch'* award notice though much briefer as the award procedures are not required. It requires the name and address of the awarding authority, a brief description of the contract in question including CPV codes, the main place of performance, number of tenders received, price or range of prices (maximum/minimum) paid, name, address and address of the successful contractor and any other relevant information. Regulation 75 (2) is of particular relevance in the current pandemic and thereafter whilst any contracts procured using urgency processes are in existence. This says that the obligation to advertise shall not apply where a negotiated procedure without prior publication of an advertisement could have been used, in accordance with regulation 32, for the award of a public service contracts. The relevant provisions of regulation 32 are regulation 32 (2) (a), which is where there have been no tenders, no suitable tenders, no requests or suitable requests to requests to participate in response to an open procedure or a restricted procedure, provided that the initial conditions of the contract are not substantially altered. Therefore, if a pre-COVID-19 pandemic contract needs some modification it is not necessary to advertise. Regulation 32

(2) (c) is probably the most relevant. This exclusion from the obligation to advertise is '*insofar as is strictly necessary where, for reasons of extreme urgency brought about by events unforeseeable by the contracting authority, the time limits for the open or restricted procedures or competitive procedures with negotiation cannot be complied with*'. There is an additional caveat in regulation 32 (4), '*... the circumstances invoked to justify extreme urgency must not in any event be attributable to the contracting authority*'. This latter exception is intended to cover short-term needs arising from the extreme urgency not to provide an alternative to the requirement to advertise or an excuse not to advertise because of forgetting to advertise. Incompetence is not excuse (see *Salt International Ltd v The Scottish Ministers [2015] CSIH 85*).

In practice, a two-stage process with a long-listing and then a short listing of a limited number of contractors is commonplace and recommended. Short listing means that contractors know they are on a list with a limited number of competitors. This encourages them to consider that it is worthwhile spending the considerable time and therefore cost required to put in a bid. These are not simple or straightforward for contractors and whilst the initial selection questionnaire stage is relatively quick for contractors to complete, the award stage is not.

Regulation 76 (3) states that 'in particular', the procurement should be carried out in accordance with the contract notice 'conditions for participation', time limits for contacting the authority; or the award procedure to be applied except in the limited circumstances as set out in regulation76 (4). This says that limited changes which are possible after the issue of the contract notice, but only if there is no breach of principles of transparency and equal treatment of contractors, the local authority has considered this issue before proceeding and given due consideration to the matter, concluded there is no breach of regulation 76 (4) (a), documented that conclusion and its reasons in accordance with regulation 84 (7) and informs participants who have responded to the notice of the respects which they intend to proceed in a way not in conformity with the notice (see regulation 76 (4) (b)).

If more extensive changes are needed a new or amended contract notice with extended time scales may be required. If a regulation process has been used and the subsequent contract notice is significantly different, the contract notice ought to allow longer for response so the changes can be taken into account by bidders.

The limitation on later changes to the procurement are particularly relevant to complex procurements like leisure and culture services and/or where it may become apparent via the clarification process during the procurement that the original documents require amendment because of responses to clarification questions.

The evaluation and award criteria may (i.e. not must) take into account a number of factors (see regulation 76 (8)) namely, the need to ensure quality, continuity, accessability, affordability, availability and comprehensiveness of services, the specific needs of different categories of users, the involvement and empowerment of users and innovation. The generality of these should all have been taken into account as part of the leisure or cultural strategy. The procurement ought to reflect the strategy and take into account its vision and objectives especially in the specification. As identified above, strategic changes may require further consultation.

A Standard Selection Questionnaire was introduced as mandatory from 8th September 2016 (see Crown Commercial Services, *Procurement Policy Note: Standard Selection Questionnaire (SQ)* Action Note 8/16 in substitution for the pre-qualification questionnaire (PQQ) process (see regulation 59). Its purpose is to set out the questions used to evaluate the contractors at this first stage, the evaluation stage which seeks information from bidders on their current and historic status including their financial and technical status. It is unclear if this questionnaire applies to '*light touch*', even the CCR guidance is unclear (see below). However, as most of the questions are standard this should be used, with any required changes.

The selection questionnaire in Wales is slightly though not materially different. In May 2018, the Welsh Government issued a procurement advice note for use when authorities are using the online ESPD (European Single Procurement Documents) on Sell2Wales to create their own document. This is said to be mandatory from October 2018 and refers to the Wales Procurement Policy Statement (dated 2014 i.e. before the PCR) which sets out the principles expected of Welsh authorities.

From 1st January 2021, there is to be a UK version which includes relevant amendments in the 2020 regulations. Guidance on this was issued by the Cabinet Office in November 2020:

Procurement Policy Note 08/20 – Introduction of Find a Tender –

https://www.gov.uk/government/publications/procurement-policy-note-0820-introduction-of-find-a-tender.

Neither sets of guidance address the issue of how to apply its requirements to 'light touch' procurements. As identified above, according to some parts of the guidance on 'light touch' issued by the Crown Commercial Office it applies to 'light touch' but this does not make sense because the underlying regulations and therefore the requirements which must be included do not apply to 'light touch'. Other parts of the guidance suggest it is a recommendation. Many of the questions are standard and in practice, the most sensible approach is to adopt this so far as it is sensible to do so.

The first procurement stage looks back at whether a contractor has the core technical leisure and culture expertise, financial and commercial status and is qualified to bid i.e. neither subject to mandatory or discretionary disqualification (for example because of insolvency or poor financial status). It is different to the award stage which considers the future ability to deliver services (see *Emm G Lianakis AE (and ors) v Alexandroupolis* ECJ C-532/06 and OGC Action Note 04/09 29 April 2009).

The governance model should also be considered in outline at this stage. This is particularly important in the leisure and culture sector. Where a contractor has recognised charitable status the governance model is relatively simple as the contract will be in the name of the charity. Where a commercial contractor sets up a model which includes a charity or non-profit distributing organisation to take advantage of the NNDR benefit applied to these structures the evaluation may be more difficult because each commercial contractor has a slightly different model, and the models are changed from time to time by contractors. There are therefore a number of marketplace variations and individual local authorities will apply reliefs in a differing manner (see chapter 11).

Both Welsh and English approaches and documents are supposed to be simpler as only the winning contractor(s) have to prove their status. They limit the information which can generally be sought, place the burden of self-certification that it can comply onto the contractor and if a winning contractor cannot later prove that it meets the pre-qualification status, it will be rejected at a very late stage after they have carried out all of the work to get approved. Whether this is good practice for 'light touch' procurements is uncertain as it may be preferable for authorities and contractors to have a standard pre-qualification process, rejecting contractors who do not meet the criteria at an early stage as part of the shortlisting process so that all who are short listed know if they have qualified. The information should be updated immediately prior to completion, for example with later accounts and even the successful contractor should be rejected at that stage if for example, there is a significant deterioration in financial status or there are other significant problems. This is pragmatic advice; it is not wholly clear whether this is compliant as a requirement within the procurement documents.

The aspect of procurement which creates the most litigation is the process for evaluating the award and how it is carried out. The award criteria and process, which should be set out in the procurement documents, set out the criteria against which each bid is to be evaluated. This must now be based on the most economically advantageous offer (MEAT) from the perspective of the authority i.e. a price : quality decision based on a sound evaluation of the published criteria (see regulation 67). This applies only to the non 'light touch' procedure. It is inconceivable that a 'light touch' procedure would be evaluated on a price only basis, without considering quality as well.

The respective weighting of each of price and quality has a profound effect on the outcome particularly because a different approach is almost always used for price and quality. There are a number of different approaches to evaluating these criteria. A commonly used example is that that the cheapest bid will receive 100% and the other bidders' a reduction in percentage depending on their bid sum. This is to be compared to the approach for the quality evaluation which is subjective. It is very rare in this sector for any bidder to receive 100%. It is sensible to spend time structuring and testing the award criteria to ensure it meets the local authority's intentions as unexpected outcomes can happen if this is not done. It is outside the scope of this book to consider it in more detail.

An aspect which can be an issue in this sector is the extent to which a contractor's past performance may be taken into account especially if this is a re-procurement. The PCR do not specifically deal with this. It is considered that it is intrinsic in regulation 76 and in particular regulation 76 (8) that these are relevant considerations. If past performance is to be used, the information which is to be gathered and how it will be used must be identified in the published evaluation or award procedure. An approach and methodology must be included to validate the accuracy of the assumptions and ensure that the process and approach complies with the requirements for equal treatment of all bidders. This should include giving bidders an opportunity of responding to comments about past performance. Information about past performance can be used information to validate other information, for example claims that the bidder achieves certain quality standards whereas references and visits to other facilities cast doubt on this. Demonstrating fairness and equal treatment of all bidders may also be difficult to achieve as an authority almost inevitably has more available information about an existing contractor.

Ideally, the award evaluation should be carried out independently of the client-side officer for the existing contract if at all possible, to avoid an allegation of conflict because of previous knowledge. History can either be positive or negative bias in favour of or against an existing contractor. There are examples of a successful challenge because of bias (see for example, *Counted4 Community Interest Company v. Sunderland City Council [2015] EWHC 3898 (TCC)*). Detailed consideration of how to carry out an award evaluation is outside the terms of reference of this book.

As identified above, regulation 74 says that the 'light touch' provisions apply to selection and award process. The implication of this is that apart from the selection and award process all other provisions of the PCR apply to 'light touch'. This is the safest interpretation to apply, though this is not wholly clear.

The modification and termination provisions are set out in regulations 72 and 73. It is assumed that they apply to '*light touch*'. They are particularly important at present and will be for some time to come because even when the immediate effects of the pandemic are over, it is likely that it will have an impact on leisure and cultural services for some time as they have been so massively affected by the pandemic. There is every likelihood that most or all leisure and cultural contracts will require modification or even termination.

Where there is a requirement for change in service during the contract period the extent of the parties' ability to make changes will depend to a significant effect on the terms of the contractual modification (or variation) provisions in the contract. Regulation 72 only allows for modifications in certain circumstances without a re-tendering. The circumstances are if this has been provided for in the original procurement documents irrespective of monitory value in *'clear, precise and unequivocal review clauses'*, provided these do not 'alter the overall nature of the contract or framework' (regulation 72 (I) (a)), for additional works 'necessary' not included in the original procurement where a change of contractor cannot be made for economic, or technical reasons e.g. inoperability (for example computer software) or would mean substantial duplication of costs provided any increase in price is not more than 50% of the value of the original contract (regulation 72 (1) (b)), where a need for a modification is caused 'by circumstances which a diligent contracting authority could not have foreseen and the modification does not affect the overall nature of the contract and any increase in price does not exceed 50% of the value of the original contract or framework (regulation 72 (1) c)) each time the contract was varied, for a replacement contractor e.g. following a company re-structuring (regulation 72 (1) (d), where the modification is below the threshold and not substantial as defined in regulation 72 (8), i.e. no other contractors would have joined the procurement (regulation 72 (1) (e)). Each modification is sequential. Regulation 73 requires that every PCR contract must contain provisions enabling termination where there is a substantial modification outside the modification provisions or there is a mandatory disqualification ground in existence.

Apart from a modification under regulation 72 (1) (a) and where urgency procedures are used (as identified above), a notice setting out details of the modification must be published with the information required in the form set out in Part G of Annex V to the Public Contracts Directive. The main information relevant to these procurements which is required is the name of the local authority, the CPV codes, the main location of the service delivery, a description of the procurement before and after the modification, the nature and extent of the services, where applicable the increase in price caused by the modification, the circumstances which have made the modification necessary, the date of contract award decision, where there is a new contractor, their name and address, whether the contract is related to a project and /or programme financed by the EU, the date(s) and reference(s) of previous publications in OJEU relevant to the contract(s) concerned by this notice, the date of the notice and any other relevant information. There is one Supreme Court case on the meaning of the modification provisions. This held that where a contract was entered into under the public contracts regulations 2006 i.e. the legislation which is now repealed, the modification provisions in the PCR 2015 applied (*Edenred (UK Group) Ltd v HM Treasury and ors. [2015] EWC 90 (QB)*). This is important in this sector because in practice where a contract was a 'Part B' service (although see above as many were always concessions) there are many contracts with some years to run which were entered into prior to 2015, which have many years to run and which do not include sophisticated variation provisions. Indeed how could they reflect a regulatory regime which was not known. This problem is also relevant to concessions (see below). These contracts may have had modification provisions which are not detailed and modifications may not be possible under regulation 72 (1) (a), if this applies. Therefore, in order to make modifications because of COVID-19 the provisions of regulation 72 (1) (c) may need to be used. This may not be sufficiently flexible even with the benefit of the PPN guidance (see below).

The remedies or challenges to the procurement processes set out in do apply (see Part 3, Remedies regulations 85 – 104) although even the government's guidance say it is unclear whether the regulations governing standstill notices apply (see regulation 86). Even though the standstill provisions may do not apply to 'light touch' it is good practice to provide the equivalent information to that required in a standstill notice to all who bid either unsuccessfully either at the shortlisting stage for those who were unsuccessful at that stage or to all the long listing stage. The required information in the notice is the criteria for the award and the reasons for the decision on a relative comparative basis, comparing the successful bid with the specific unsuccessful bidder's bid. If the contract has not been entered into it cannot be entered into unless the standstill is lifted by the court. There are strict time scales for challenging an award or a modification notice. Proceedings should be started as soon as possible with a time scale of 30 days, three months with consent of the court or six months for a declaration of ineffectiveness from the date the contract was entered into. The time scales apply from the date that the organisation first knew or ought to have known of the right to challenge, which may be many months before the bidder is unsuccessful. Detailed consideration of the issues and case law is outside the scope of this book.

Sound Approaches to Procurement and Processes for Leisure and Culture, Where the CCR is Relevant

This section considers the procurement rules and procedures for concession contracts. As identified above, pre-COVID-19 most '*light touch*' procurements were concession contracts. It is also likely that most post COVID-19 procurements will also be concessions. Whilst contractors may be unwilling to take all or even some income risk in the short-term post COVID-19, as the market recovers it is envisaged that this will change and on whole life analysis of the contractual terms for longer contract there will be a transfer of income and other risk and therefore a concession.

The government has said that the CCR were based on the PCR. There are significant similarities and differences from the PCR though, even compared to the regulatory regime which applies for the different procedures. The general rules for concession contracts are less prescriptive than for public contracts and a '*light touch*' concession procurement has even less prescription than other concession contracts.

Wherever possible in this section, any repetition of similar provisions is avoided by use of references to the section on the PCR. Where the regime for a concession contract including a '*light touch*' procurement and the provisions for post award modifications have significant differences and the main differences these are identified.

As identified above, a concession is valued on the value of the contract to the contractor/concessionaire not the payment to the contractor. The threshold for a '*light touch*' is the same as that for all other concessions. The CCR claim to be specific about the regulations which apply to a '*light touch*' concession whereas the PCR are not similarly specified. '*Concession contracts for social and other specific services listed in Schedule 3 falling within the scope of these Regulations shall be subject only to the obligations arising from regulations 24(2), 31(3) to (5), 32 and 46 to 64*' (see regulation 19). The implications of this in relation to structuring a good or best practice concession process and managing the contract thereafter is identified below.

The claim that the provisions are specific in identifying only those provisions which apply to '*light touch*' does not make linguistic or other sense in all instances. It is outside the scope of this section to identify all of the difficulties as some are not specifically relevant to '*light touch*' concession procurements but there are some difficulties of interpretation which are identified.

Regulation 31 is about award, in particular the provisions that identify the regulations which apply to the commencement of a concession. It should be commenced by a PIN which includes the information set out in Annex VI to the concessions directive and sent for publication in accordance with regulation 33. This is substantially the same as the information required for PCR contracts though briefer. The reference to the description of the contact/concession and its value is expressed slightly differently as '*Description of the services, indicative order of magnitude or value*'. This is a reflection of the different nature of a concession compared to a PCR contract.

Regulation 31(5) refers to publication in accordance with regulation 33, this is not expressed as applying to '*light touch*' concessions, which does not make sense.

In addition, there is no equivalent to regulation 32 (1) c) in the PCR which provides for an award without advertisement for urgent '*light touch*' concessions. In any event Regulation 31 (6) which is the broad equivalent of regulation 32 of the PCR, covering the flexibilities for failed procurements or those where there is only one suitable contractor etc. does not apply to '*light touch*' concessions. Provisions dealing with special rules for urgent concessions are absent from the *concessions directive* so as the UK legislation simply follows the directive there is a lack of clarity in the case of urgent concession procurement.

The reason is not specified in any guidance or otherwise. It is possible to speculate about why this is the case, for example, it may well be because of the much higher thresholds for concessions which mean that the European Commission considered that the threshold would enable short-term urgent contracts to be let which are below the CCR threshold. Whatever the reason, this could well be a practical problem in letting even a short-term contract if an existing contractor fails. The turnover of many leisure centre contracts is significantly in excess of the threshold in any twelve months and a full leisure or culture procurement takes a minimum of twelve months, usually eighteen months and as much as two years to deliver. The outcome of this is that all concessions in excess of the threshold, namely a total value to the concessionaire of £4,733,252 must be advertised in accordance with the CCR.

Regulation 32 deals with award notices and provides for notification of award notices within 48 days of award with specific rules for *'light touch'* awards, which may be grouped and identification that the notice must be in the form set out with the information required in Annex VIII of the concessions directive. The approach is similar to that for *'light touch'* under the PCR, the differences reflecting the different nature of a concession. Therefore, there is a requirement to set out the *'Value of the successful tender, including fees and prices'*.

Regulation 20 applies to mixed procurements, those which consist of both works and services, although it is not referred to in the list of regulations which apply to *'light touch'*. Where there is a mixed contract, *'the main subject matter shall be determined in accordance with which of the estimated values of the respective services is the highest'* (regulation 20 (2)). It is therefore essential to carry out a careful valuation before the commencement of the procurement.

The only other provisions which are expressed as applying to *'light touch'* are the remedies provisions in regulations 46 – 64. These include the requirement to notify candidate and tenderer of the award with the standard detailed reasons for the award to the successful tenderer. There is also a requirement to have a standstill period although award notices can be notified quarterly. As identified, it is unclear if this is required for *'light touch'* contracts entered into under the PCR (though good practice). This is an example of the CCR being different to the PCR. All of the provisions relating to duties owed to tenderers and enforcement through the courts are a requirement for *'light touch'* concessions, no different to *'light touch'* contracts under the PCR.

This leaves whole swathes of the provisions which do not apply. The practical implications of this are unclear for practitioners. Government guidance, the *Handbook for the Concession Contracts Regulations 2016*, published by the Crown Commercial Service at *https://assets.publishing.service.gov.uk/government/uploads/system/uploads/attachment_data/file/528062/20160607_Handbook_for_the_Concession_Contracts_Regulations_2016_final.pdf* does not provide any assistance about good practice for *'light touch'* procurement and there is no authoritative guidance on this, though there are some historic and post the CCR emerging cases. These include the CCR case *Lancashire Care NHS Foundation Trust & Blackpool Teaching Hospitals NHS Foundation Trust v Lancashire County Council [2018] EWHC 1589 (TCC)*. The Trust, which was the existing provider of the service challenged the outcome of a procurement for services for children and young people. The award was set aside because of irregularities in the evaluation and therefore scoring processes. There was a failure to provide proper reasons for the scores i.e. the evaluation process was significantly flawed. The case law assists in identifying aspects of bad practice, not necessarily what is a good practice procurement process under the CCR.

There are no specific procedures required for the design of the procurement of a concession contract. Regulations 8 and 41 set out the key principles and award criteria. The principle of equal treatment, non-discrimination and transparency apply and (setting out below key provisions only), also that the *'design of the award procedure, including the estimate of the value, shall not be made with the intention of excluding it from the scope of these Regulations or of unduly favouring or disadvantaging certain economic operators or certain works, supplies or services'* (regulation 8). They should therefore be objective criteria which comply with the principles' in regulation 8 and *'shall be linked to the subject-matter of the concession contract'* (regulation 41). As neither of these apply to *'light touch'* concession contracts, it is unclear what award procedures local authorities should design. On a careful analysis of European principles, the requirements to be included in the PIN and award notices and a review of the *Handbook* referred to above, it is possible to identify key aspects of good practice and some implications of these on the ability to modify/vary a *'light touch'* concession.

Whilst not identified as applying the requirement to *'treat economic operators equally and without discrimination'* and *'act in a transparent and proportionate manner'* (see regulation 8) are TFEU requirements. The *concession contracts directive* makes this clear (see *Introduction paragraph (4)* and so does the *Handbook* (paragraph 1.4). Publishing a transparent process which will be followed and following this would seem basic requirements. Just as for *'light touch'* PCR contracts adopting procedures which to an extent mirror the standard CCR procedures, albeit with some flexibility rather than creating new procedures is prudent as these are tried and tested. In any event, in the case law on challenges such as the Supreme Court in *Edenred* on modifications (see above) focus on the principles in the TFEU, taking these and the directives as their starting point. This is because any UK regulations which were in derogation of these was a breach of EU law and therefore of UK law. The 2020 regulations confirm that this will still be the position for existing UK law post 31st December 2020.

The available flexibility to modify or vary a *'light touch'* concession contract is also unclear. Regulation 43, which deals with modification/variation provisions, is not identified as applying to *'light touch'*. Therefore a *'light touch'* modification does not require publication of a notice under the directive or CCR. The reason why is unclear and seems perverse as the award procedures do apply. The provisions of regulation 43 closely mirror those of regulations 72 and 73 of the PCR.

It will be seen from the above that there are a number of unresolved issues in relation to *'light touch'* leisure and culture procurements, issues which likely to be are exacerbated by the problems of COVID-19 and the lack of case law.

Consideration of some of the General, Practical and Policy Issues

As identified above, the law and their practice are complex and the *'light touch'* regime provides a local authority with considerable choice about how to carry out a leisure and culture procurement.

This choice should include consideration of what it intends to procure and why it is making specific choices. As part of the pre-procurement consideration the authority should consider the various alternative options and whether some of these should be reflected in variant bids. The terms of the procurement and specific terms and conditions of the procurement documents including the contract, specification and lease(s) will reflect the policy decisions.

As identified, there is a mature market for these services. This does not mean that all projects are similar or that they are all easy. Every project differs and has some characteristics which are specific to the individual authority. There is considerable diversity throughout the United Kingdom. Some is based on demographic and other factors which cannot easily be changed, for example population density. Others reflect the nature of local government and the way leisure and culture has developed in a particular area. Understanding the fixed points or those which cannot easily be changed and the aspects of the project which are the variables depending on how the procurement is carried out and the choice of contractor are an essential part of planning and drafting the procurement documents. This distinction is not always fully understood at all levels.

Examples of fixed points are the number, condition and geographic location of the facilities. This issue is explored in greater detail in chapter 5. Variable factors include the contract length and, for example, whether the outcome of a fixed longer contract period will result in a better value revenue payment, the commercial implications of a portfolio which has uneconomic aspects for example a leisure centre with very low usage in a poor condition, a museum and/or a small community theatre and/or services which must be delivered free or at a subsidised cost to unwaged at peak times. The impact of this on the procurement project must be understood. Some services and activities may be important town centre regenerators and improve the health and wellbeing of the area but reduce headline income.

This tension between competing local authority agendas including the political agenda, the need to reduce the headline financial cost of leisure and the role of leisure as an important driver in general economic regeneration and improving health and wellbeing are good examples of potentially inconsistent objectives.

The local authority may not understand the headline financial implications of its policy decisions. One approach to enabling this to be shown may be to allow bidders include a limited number variant bids which are intended to demonstrate the revenue implications of specific initiatives and choices. This allows the local authority to consider if it can or wants to afford these.

Conclusion

The application of the current and historic public procurement regulations, guidance and case law is not easy especially as this is such a complex area of law and practice. The PCR and CCR are unsatisfactory law because of their complexity, the number of unanswered issues and their continuing application even though the UK has left the EU. This is a code of law based on European not UK principles and it is disappointing that it will be some considerable time, possibly years, before the law changes.

The impact of the current and historic law is likely to last for many years even if the PCR and CCR are abolished because of the large number of contracts based on it.

CHAPTER SEVEN

COVID-19: THE PPN RESPONSE AND POST-COVID CONTRACTING

Introduction

This section considers government guidance on the procurement impact of COVID-19 on leisure and culture contracts and in particular, the ability of local authorities to modify or vary contracts. This will include consideration of the guidance within the PPNs, published by the Crown Commercial Service and in particular use of urgency procedures and ability to make modifications because of the pandemic.

At present, leisure and cultural contracts are at risk of failure because of COVID-19. As identified, the various requirements to close facilities and cease activity at times since March 2020 which differed at times in different parts of the county are an obvious problem but this is only part of the problem. Equally significant problems are the direct long-term impact of social distancing on the contractor's or other provider's ability to manage the relevant facility and any long-term impact on income arising from longer term economic issues. As leisure and cultural activities are discretionary spend it is unclear how quickly these activities will recover, if they do recover in the foreseeable future even when all post COVID-19 restrictions have been lifted. Income assumptions may not be able to be met during the remainder contract period for many of the contracts which are currently in existence or at least not for some years and contractors could be at risk of insolvency for a number of years to come. None of this is currently clear.

As identified in chapter 6. under existing contracts income risk is a risk which has hitherto been transferred to the contractor. The significance of this is that although the public procurement notes issued by the Cabinet Office appear to be time limited, some at least of the guidance provided in these PPNs may be relevant for some years to come.

The guidance and its implications

Guidance has been issued both by the European Commission and the Cabinet Office, on behalf of the UK Government. This is all non-mandatory guidance and does not therefore change the law. It is also general guidance and not tailored for any specific service. In particular it is based on the PCR, not the CCR. It identifies that regulation 32 (2) c) of the PCR, the provision which as identified above enables use of negotiated procedure without an advertisement process. However, most leisure contracts are currently concessions and, as identified above, there is no equivalent in the CCR.

Whilst this guidance is of limited assistance it is nevertheless useful as background information as it identifies the extent to which the Government considers flexibility is appropriate because of COVID-19. The extent to which it is of assistance in interpreting modifications for concessions in particular is unclear as is how far the courts would be prepared to consider it in any subsequent litigation on COVID-19 modifications. Nevertheless no book on local authority leisure would be complete without reference to this and a brief explanation. Whilst the guidance is listed in full below it is followed by analysis of those aspects which are likely to be particularly relevant.

The current relevant COVID-19 guidance is as follows:

Guidance from the European Commission on using the public procurement framework in the emergency situation related to the COVID-19 crisis, (2020/C 108 I/01) (April 1st 2020).

Procurement Policy Note 01/20: Responding to COVID-19 (March 18th 2020) (https://www.gov.uk/government/publications/procurement-policy-note-0120- responding-to-COVID-19).

Procurement Policy Note 02/20: Supplier relief due to COVID-19 (20th March 2020) (https://www.gov.uk/government/publications/procurement-policy-note-0220-supplier- relief-due-to-COVID-19).

Procurement Policy Note 4/20: Recovery and Transition from COVID-19 https://assets.publishing.service.gov.uk/government/uploads/system/up-loads/attachment_data/file/891154/PPN_04_20-_Recovery_and_Transition_from_COVID-19.pdf

Model Interim Payment Terms March 2020 Guidance notes on Model Interim Payment Terms -Procurement Policy Note 02/20

https://assets.publishing.service.gov.uk/government/uploads/system/up-loads/attach-ment_data/file/877260/PPN02_20_Model_Interim_Payment_Terms_v1.pdf

Frequently Asked Questions (FAQs) -Procurement Policy Note 02/20 (April)

https://assets.publishing.service.gov.uk/government/uploads/system/up-loads/attachment_data/file/879956/PPN_02_20_FAQs_09_04_20.pdf

Guidance on responsible contractual behaviour in the performance and enforcement of contracts impacted by the COVID-19 emergency (May)

https://www.gov.uk/government/publications/guidance-on-responsible-con-tractual-behaviour-in-the-performance-and-enforcement-of-contracts-im-pacted-by-the-COVID-19-emergency

No new guidance has been published on COVID-19 since *PPN 4/20* on 25th June 2020.

The UK guidance followed guidance from the EU which is only referred to in outline. Key points in the guidance from the EU are that contracting authorities can; substantially reduce the deadlines to accelerate open or restricted procedures; use negotiated procedures without publication, if necessary; use a direct award to a pre-selected contractor if there is only one able to deliver the required services within the required constraints imposed by the extreme urgency; engage with the market and seek innovative solutions; use existing call-off or purchasing arrangements. This latter may be relevant if a local authority has more than one leisure contractor. Although this is not commonplace it can happen if there is a local trust for some facilities whereas others have been more recently procured via an open market procurement. The EU say that the public procurement rules provide all the necessary tools to meet extreme urgency. It is unclear how far is true and will be of any particular relevance after 1st January except to the extent that the UK guidance echoes this.

The UK guidance echoes this. *PPN 01/20* states: that this must be genuine extreme urgency. As identified, extreme urgency is because of the circumstances and not because the authority has forgotten to go to the market or do something (see *Salt International Ltd v The Scottish Ministers [2015] CSIH 85* referred to above); local authorities should keep a written justification of using this approach; only do what is absolutely necessary both what is being procured and the length of the contract; should continue to achieve value for money and use good commercial judgement including obtaining approval for any abnormally high pricing by its section 151 officer and seek future price reductions, if possible.

The guidance also states that authorities can extend or modify a contract during its terms, although as this does not provide any statutory relief from the restrictions in the TFEU, PCR and CCR if the terms of the local authority's specific contract do not allow for this. It is unclear how far the contract terms can be properly overridden. *PPN 2/20* refers specifically to the provisions of regulation 72 of the PCR and frames the guidance within the context of this regulation, which as identified, will not apply to most existing leisure contracts because they are concessions. Similarly, whilst *PPN 4*, identifies the possible need for contracts to be foreshortened, possibly ended or otherwise amended it does not address the legal implications of any of this. The implications for leisure and cultural contracts are particularly extreme because of the likely long-term impact of COVID-19. Whilst service delivery may eventually be normalised, as identified, the impact of the pandemic on income is likely to last for a considerable time.

There are some important comments within the guidance, e.g. the local authority should expect to pay compensation for claims arising from COVID-19 but not otherwise. The whole thrust of the guidance is that sums can be made to secure service or business continuity in relation to COVID-19 difficulties and should not be used to prop up a business or a contractual relationship which was failing or subject to contractual claims pre-COVID-19.

Suppliers should not expect to make profits on contract elements which are not delivered. The guidance is blank on whether contractors can make profits on those elements which are delivered. Suppose the contract is not easily divisible, for example a leisure contract where social distancing requirements mean that only 50% occupancy is possible but profitability is based on a much higher level of occupancy what is the implication? This is another example of lack of clarity of thinking and where local authorities will have to make up their own minds on a pragmatic basis.

Contractors should not make multiple duplicate claims, for example they cannot furlough staff and claim for their salaries. The *PPNs* say records should be kept and there should be responsible and fair behaviour (see above) with open book accounting. This is all aspirational. There is a recognition that contractors are likely to become less robust and may be at risk of failing because of COVID-19. This places local authorities in a 'chicken and egg' situation whereby they have make a payment to secure contract continuity but have no guarantee that this will protect them from contractor failure. As all of this is only guidance, not statutory guidance, its use will be fact specific and dependent on the individual relationships, status and strength of any particular contractor. It is very possible that there will be litigation if not in this sector in other sectors by dissatisfied competitors shut out of profitable urgent contract.

As identified, there are guidance notes and model interim payment terms. These terms are overly wordy and ideally, ought to be simplified before they are used. A formal modification or variation will however, be needed in most if not all instances even where any payment is made strictly in accordance with contractual risk share arrangements.

Using urgency procedure by direct negotiation may avoid the need to send an award notice (see regulation 86 (5)). What happens if you are in the middle of a procurement and need to procure urgently, can you just change the criteria and proceed with the procurement on different terms accepting this is not transparent or should you use the urgency process to justify a short-term procured solution, abandon the procurement and revert to it on a different basis post the pandemic? This will be a fact specific decision.

There is now some guidance on how far the *PPNs* will be used by the courts in guiding their approach to post COVID-19 contract interpretation in the 2021 Westminster case referred to above. The approach of the parties and of Kerr J in that case was to consider the terms of the contract and not the *PPNs* so it is fair to say that these may be of very limited or no interpretive value. It is still unclear how far, if at all, local authorities' external auditors and council tax payers will investigate or challenge decisions taken during the pandemic and the impact of this is for the future and could remain an issue for some years to come

Future Government Proposals for Public Procurement

On 15th December, the Government published a Green Paper, *Transforming public procurement*

(*https://assets.publishing.service.gov.uk/government/uploads/system/uploads/attachment_data/file/944196/CCS001_CCS1020400576-001_Transforming_Public_Procurement_WebAccessible_1_.pdf*) for consultation. Its expressed objective is to *'Overhaul our outdated public procurement regime'* (Ministerial Forward). It is to be a fundamental review of the approach to public procurement in this country. The consultation period will last until 10th March 2021, though if the recommendations within the Green Paper are accepted it will mean the abolition of 'light touch' as part of a general simplification of the law. It will though be some considerable time before there are any significant changes to the law and it is unclear how far these will affect contracts procured under the current law with modification provisions based on this.

CHAPTER EIGHT

TERMS AND CONDITIONS FOR THE CONTRACT (INCLUDING THE SPECIFICATION)

Introduction

This chapter considers the specific contractual requirements for leisure and cultural contracts and the terms and conditions which are required to implement these. These will have several aspects, they should reflect the policy decisions and outcome of the procurement decisions as identified in chapters 4 and 6. In addition, they will include a number of standard or 'boiler plate' terms and conditions and provide the 'wrapper' for the specification and other technical schedules and appendix. As identified, the contract is the key document governing the relationship throughout the contract period.

As identified, there is a mature market for these services. There are also some 'industry standard' positions in particular areas. When drafting the contract, the local authority's officers who are involved in the drafting need to understand these standard positions which ought to be reflected in the draft contract included with the procurement documents. Negotiation is unlikely to be successful in changing these and including different provisions runs the risk of extensive clarification questions and conditional bids.

The local authority also needs to understand those aspects which can and should be negotiated as they will depend on variable factors. It is essential that all officers involved in the procurement and also elected members (where matters are of political importance) and not only the local authority's solicitors understand the commercial and practical matters underpinning the drafting of the contract. This is true whether or not the authority is carrying out the drafting and/or other work (such as procurement and specification) in-house, using standard documents and/or using external advisors. It is the local authority which manages the contract thereafter and not any advisors.

As identified in chapter 6, there may be the opportunity to include variable bids which are later reflected in the contract as in contract changes. An example of this is whether the local authority will pay for fitness equipment upgrades on a specific cyclical basis or offer a longer contract as a commitment rather than as a possibility and another example is whether the contract can or will be varied to exclude an uneconomic facility during the contract period.

Another factor which must be understood is that although the relationship may be badged as a partnership, in reality all contractual and even grant based relationships are commercial. The parties have some common interests but also have different commercial interests. That does not mean the relationship should be adversarial; it should be collaborative, it means that the relationship should be built on a sensible commercial basis and it is essential that the contract is properly drafted and reflects the best commercial position which is achievable.

The above is the backdrop to this consideration of contract terms and their meaning and implications, risks and their transfer.

A snapshot of the key provisions to be included within a well drafted contract is set out below. This includes an overview of the provisions which are likely to require particular consideration and may be controversial. This section is intended to identify the specific contract issues relevant to leisure and culture procurement. There is no consideration of general contractual provisions which do not have any specific leisure or cultural implications nor of topics such as format and drafting style.

The Contract Terms

There are a number of market-place standard precedent terms and conditions, industry standard, individual advisors' variants of these and examples of use by local authorities of their own terms and conditions modified for a leisure and/or cultural procurement. The intention in this chapter is to support and assist local authorities and those who contract with them in identifying and understanding the issues which underpin, inform and govern these specific terms and conditions for both contracts and leases. All standard terms and conditions must be customised and understood each time they are used. This is made clear in the guidance to and drafting of industry standard terms, they are not intended to be used without this and nor can they be as clauses sometimes include alternatives. Where an authority uses its own standard terms customising is even more important as these may be designed for very different services. Where standard terms are used without understanding the commercial meaning of individual provisions or the process of customising is not carried out effectively there are likely to be later difficulties during the delivery of the contract which can be commercially significant.

As identified, standard terms and conditions should never be used without understanding the rationale behind the terms and conditions, the meaning of individual provisions and the alternatives which are identified. This latter is particularly important as discussion of alternatives can often be glossed over in view of tight time scales. In addition, no standard terms and conditions can ever be fully up-to-date, later changes in the law and practice must be taken into account and must be reflected in the drafting. The end of the EU exit transition period has meant that the current period is a time of particular change.

This section will include identifying the main provisions which are required in a leisure and/or cultural procurement, focussing on the former. It will include consideration of the various approaches to specifications, payment options and other matters.

A recent and obvious example of the requirement to be nimble in understanding the implications of recent events is the impact of COVID-19 on the leisure and cultural sector.

There are two basic issues when drafting for the future, what should the contract say, for example about variations/modifications, change of law risk and force majeure and how far the turmoil caused by the pandemic will affect the commercial terms and risks which the market will accept in respect of these and many other matters.

As identified in the section on property, it is usual for the contract to be the primary document and for it to include all payment provisions together, in most instances, with the management arrangements for the property.

In this section there are separate paragraphs on specific contract terms and conditions as set out below.

Contract Length: this ought to reflect the nature of the contract. Any contract fetters the discretion of the relevant local authority to change the arrangements and so contract length should be as short as appropriate to reflect whether or not there is any contractor investment, the nature of the portfolio, whether the local authority considers it will need to change the portfolio during the contract period and the most economic and value for money contractual revenue payments. If there is no substantial contractor investment the contract should be shorter as, for example there is no need or value in fettering discretion for 20 years plus. If this is a PFI or other contract with substantial contractor investment which has to be secured against the contract period and written down during this, the contract period may be upwards of 25 years. Whilst the market may want as long as possible to secure a valuable contract and it is commercially sensible for there to be a reasonable contract length to allow the market to recoup its procurement costs within the contract payment (thus supporting best value), leisure and local government are fast changing so too long a contract period is not recommended. A reasonable period which allows the successful contractor to recover the transaction costs in bidding and to develop the services is likely to be 10 or possibly 15 years maximum with the possibility of a break.

Contract Payment (or Operating Fee): historically the local authority paid the provider the net difference between income and cost to manage the facilities. However, in the years prior to COVID-19 there were an increasing number of local authority areas where the contractor made a net surplus and paid the local authority. Historically, all income risk from users would be the contractor's risk. Post COVID-19 the commercial basis of these transfers is likely to change and until facility usage and therefore income recovers a net surplus and payment from the contractor to the local authority is not likely in most instances. It is also unclear how far the market will accept all income risk in the future. The commercial basis of leisure procurement and service delivery will therefore change and so therefore will the terms for such transactions. This issue interrelates with change of law provisions and is a current uncertainty.

Surplus share: some contracts include this seeking to ensure that the contractor does not make a windfall profit if income is greater than envisaged, others do not as the local authority may take the view that to do so could depress the contract payment which is offered and they are very unlikely to achieve any significant payment. This is a matter for commercial consideration in each instance.

Change of law: whilst there are a number of alternative marketplace positions on responsibility for change of law, the position in many commercially negotiated and other contracts is that general change of law (the changes which affect all industries) will be the responsibility of the contractor and specific change of law (the legislation which is industry specific and for example, required leisure and cultural buildings to close because of COVID-19 and once open to operate on a reduced basis) will be the responsibility of the local authority. The contract should provide for mitigation and payment should be net of expenditure saved because facilities cannot open including for example furlough payments. It should also be net of profit. The change of law payment structure will be part of the modification/variation process. In practice most contracts (though not all) will need be drafted on the basis that the majority of contractual COVID-19 risk sits with the local authority but the contractor makes no profit and so also bears risk and cost. In a well drafted contract this is likely to be similar to the Government's *PPN* guidance (see chapter 7). This is potentially a contentious issue with very significant financial implications for both local authorities and contractors as demonstrated by the case referred to above, *Westminster City Council v Sports and Leisure Management Ltd [2021 EWC 98 (TCC)*. This case was about a contract with a management fee or contract payment which was made by the contractor to the local authority and whether post COVID-19 it could ever be negative i.e. a payment by the local authority to the contractor. The decision turned on the interpretation of a contract based on standard terms where the Judge commented that the words used in the contract were *'imperfectly drafted'*. It was held that the terms meant there could be no negative payment so whilst the management fee was waived, the contractor's claim for a COVID-19 claim of more than that failed. Whilst each claim will turn on its own terms, the implications of the case are clearly commercially very significant.

Specification, services standards and contract management: these sets of provisions should interrelate although they may be in different places within the contract. The majority of specifications in this sector are a mixture of inputs and outputs. The specification ought to identify the services which are required at the beginning of the contract, though there may well be regular changes to these during the contract period. These reviews may be often based around annual quality assurance meetings. The contractual arrangements for quality assurance and service reviews should dovetail in with the outputs required under the specification. The overall terms will reflect the extent to which the authority wants to control what is delivered including the opening hours, subsidised usage and manage the relationship closely or less closely. There may be a tension between the freedom requested by the contractor and which the contractor may argue is needed to offer the best value contract payment and the desire to require relatively tight control of services because these are local community facilities. Effective modern contractual relationships in this sector are built on the contractor achieving identified performance standards, which will be flexible and change with service changes. The standards which are achieved will be sent to the local authority's contract manager at regular intervals to be should be discussed at the regular contract meetings (quarterly, annually and sometimes monthly) on the basis that the contractor and not the local authority carries out the collection of the indicators and demonstrates achievement of the quality assurance plan. There are industry standard systems accreditation systems, such as Quest though some local authorities and contractors prefer to agree their own approach. Ideally, the relationship ought to be based on a collaborative rather than an adversarial approach as, although the contract will include requirements to provide service improvement plans, default and even termination clauses, these ought to be a last and not a first resort as by the time they are invoked the relationship will probably already have broken down.

Partnership board: some local authorities seek to include specific arrangements for partnership working involving the community and other key stakeholders such as health as part of the service management and review and may even include a partnership fund. This possibility is a matter for the local authority, some of these are successful and others add little or no value and fail to function.

Variations: these are known as modifications in the PCR and CCR and change management provisions in some contracts. The provisions in the PCR and CCR regarding variations, are set out in chapter 6. The importance of well drafted variation clauses which seek to predict likely future events and provide for them in precise language cannot be overstated, however difficult this is to achieve. General variation clauses whilst historically common are no longer effective in view of the changes to the public procurement legislation. Leisure and culture services are likely to change during the contract period as these services are to an extent fashion services where changing public interest and habits and leisure equipment mean that flexibility in service delivery is essential. The regular changes in the specification, referred to above and often based around the annual meetings referred should be distinguished from more significant changes to facilities including changes to the portfolio (for example if a facility is no longer fit for purpose and is either to be closed or replaced). Some contracts envisage transformation in the early years or more extensive review after a specific time, for example the contract midpoint or as part of a pre-extension discussion. If so, these provisions including potentially no-fault termination provisions need to be sign posted and drafted within the contract. All of the above requires the variation provisions to specify the process for the implementation of modifications or change management in as much detail as possible. If this is not identified in detail, there may be commercial and procurement difficulties in achieving the required change (see chapter 6).

Insurance, indemnities and damages: all of these are a necessary part of any contract and unexceptional in principle. Specific requirements for these services include whether or not to insist on business interruption insurance and if this is included the impact on payment of damages to the contractor for loss of income due to the local authority's failure, for example because a building is not repaired. A further issue which can be contentious is the extent to which a provider wants damages capped, the level of cap and whether the local authority is prepared to comply.

Force majeure: force majeure is a contractual remedy. Unlike a concept such as repudiation, a force majeure clause only applies if and to the extent it is included. A force majeure clause enables the parties to avoid specified contractual requirements if there is an unexpected no fault event for example a pandemic. The outcome of this is that there will be no requirement for the contract to be delivered. Until COVID-19 force majeure clauses were included as a matter of routine without there necessarily being much thought behind them and may not be have been sufficiently sophisticated to cope with the pressures of the pandemic. There may well be no provisions in the existing arrangements to allow for termination because of force majeure arising from COVID-19 (or for any other no-fault reason) although this may be agreed to as being sensible by both parties. This may mean that termination is not possible (see chapter 6). The provisions the parties ought to include in new contracts relating an event of force majeure which may make the contract uneconomic is likely to be given much more thought, though at present there is no standard market position. The pandemic has brought this into the forefront of the parties' minds. The clause may or may not enable the contract to end on a no-fault basis. Payment provisions and other obligations will cease.

Fees and Charges: section 19 Local Government (Miscellaneous Provisions) Act 1976 requires the local authority to have control over fees and charges, although this can be light touch. In practice some local authorities may want approve core fees and charges each year (via a member process or decision delegated to officers). Fees and charges are likely to increase annually by inflation. There is variation between the approach of different local authorities, some wish to protect subsidised services for certain categories of users, for example, the unwaged, children and young people, older people, members of the forces and those with disabilities, others are not concerned about this. In Wales, there is a greater, although reducing, level of subsidies for example for Key stage 4 swimming for children and older people. The local authority needs to decide what it wants to achieve, recognising the tension between requiring subsidised activities, overall income and therefore the net cost of the services. Whilst the contractor market recognises that these are community activities, nevertheless freedom to set charges is their preference. This allows them to seek to increase income wherever possible based on the market and set fees and charges which seek to achieve this.

Intellectual property, leisure card and database: one issue which is of considerable importance, particularly at the beginning and end of the contract is transfer of membership and other information. The new contractor/service provider requires this information to continue to deliver the services with no member leakage and yet under the Data Protection Act 2018 and requirements of GDPR it may be a breach of the law if this information is transferred without consent. The position will be fact specific and it is outside the scope of this book except to say that early consideration of this is essential.

Provisions for the end of the contract: a well drafted contract will include detailed provisions addressing the end of contract arrangements including transfer of assets, memberships and people however the contract ends. HR and TUPE is dealt with in more detail in chapter 10.

Utilities: the cost of utilities, particularly where there is a swimming pool(s), is one of the significant contractor costs. Utility costs have been very volatile in recent years and are a cost which neither party can control effectively although effective management can reduce cost. There are a number of alternative market positions. Where a service was transferred to a NPDO, which is intrinsically VAT inefficient and which has limited ability to access the best procurement terms for utilities, the position may have been that the local authority kept responsibility for the provision and payment of utilities. The disadvantage to this has been that there is no incentive for the NPDO to be frugal. In view of this, market positions have developed which either splits risk or transfers it to the contractor historically. This issue needs consideration as part of the procurement planning and delivery.

_____

CHAPTER NINE

PROPERTY

Introduction

This chapter considers a number of separate property aspects of leisure and culture projects. It is split into several sections which include the general property aspects and the specific terms and conditions for the disposal of property within these projects.

To be sustainable and sound the terms must be based on a model that is acceptable to the local authority together with its existing and prospective contractor/providers. Whilst it may have been possible to externalise to a new trust on terms which the commercial contractors would not have accepted (though this may have long term consequences for both parties in any procurement) if the terms are not acceptable to the market, the number of bidders will be reduced and/or those who do bid may not participate or will not do so at an affordable price. Only a model which reflects the optimum approach will achieve the best outcome. The cost of accepting property risk can be considerable for the private sector and COVID-19 is likely to make the market more risk averse. Understanding the optimum model of property risk retention and transfer is essential.

The impact of COVID-19 on future property models is unclear. COVID-19 has been a massive shock for all in this market. The different property models for current and historic transactions are set out against the background of recent events.

Why is Property so Important?

Leisure and culture are property-based services. With some very limited exceptions, these services cannot be delivered except from buildings. The main exceptions are some park-based activities, playing fields and sports development. These latter are a very small commercial part of the overall services. If they are relevant they can be included within the service specification and management arrangements within the contract. The buildings-based property aspects are of fundamental importance. The position, condition, number, size and type of facilities within the portfolio are key drivers.

More is not necessarily better and nor are facilities necessarily of positive commercial or operational value, something which can be an unwelcome surprise for a local authority. When evaluating a bidding opportunity leisure and culture service providers consider the overall portfolio and the extent to which they can add value/income to each facility and/or service. A large number of facilities which may not be at the centre of populations, have little or no parking, are in a poor state of repair, do not have full access for people with disabilities and require significant numbers of staff all of which are disproportionate to the income which can be achieved, can depress interest in the procurement.

The current optimum commercial position is considered in this chapter, some consideration of the implications of the history is also considered as it is still directly relevant today. As identified in chapter 5, the market has developed considerably since the early days and there are still a significant, though diminishing number of older projects based on the trust model where the provider delivers services under a lease with or without a separate grant agreement.

The Current Marketplace and Legacy of the Past on Property Aspects

There was a building boom in building indoor leisure facilities by local authorities from the nineteen sixties through to the nineteen eighties. Many of the facilities built forty or more years ago have reached or exceeded their life and not fit for current patterns of service delivery. They may be in poor physical condition, a condition exacerbated by local authority budget cuts preventing regular and timely repair including the replacement of roofs, boilers, electrical wiring, pool floors, tiling or the fitness equipment. They may not provide for full access to people with disabilities. Major refurbishment may cost more than re-building because the buildings are based on an out-of-date design and will still be expensive to run and require upkeep but the local authority may have no money to do either. Facilities which are forty or more years old and in a poor state of repair may be much loved and/or the only facility in a specific community or not able to compete with the private sector or with low budget and other competitors.

Even before COVID-19 this was a problem in-spite of a new-build programme within a number of local authorities based often on grant funding e.g. from Sport England plus prudential borrowing. Post COVID-19 the requirement for social distancing has exacerbated existing difficulties e.g. that older facilities built by predecessor local authorities, even when they are in good condition they may not allow for social distancing, may be too small to be economically viable and/or built in the wrong place.

The outcome is an impossible problem for local authorities and its providers. There may be facilities which either cannot open in the short term or are and will be so uneconomic to open that providers cannot afford to do so and local authorities cannot afford to pump more money into the service.

In some instances, where all of the income risk is with the contractor, contractors are saying that they cannot open facilities and are seeking to agree variations or termination clauses. However, as identified in chapters 6 and 8 there may not be suitable break clauses in leases and contracts and as identified in the *Westminster* case the contractor may have negotiated terms which in retrospect are uneconomic. This s a current problem faced by local authorities and the industry and requires a case-by-case approach and solution.

Historic Patterns of Property Disposal and What We Have Learned From This

Historic patterns of property disposal and funding are important for some local authorities because they survive to this day in some areas and because they are essential in understanding the development of the market.

The structure of some of the early transfers to newly created trusts in the 1990s was based on a newly created trust being given long leases of 20 years plus potentially with full or substantial repairing obligations. In the early years, as there were no tried and tested precedents different local authorities, their in-house professionals and their advisors had different views about the preferred length of a service transfer and detail of the legal model including the property structure. Some local authorities thought unrealistically that their properties were assets and had unrealistic expectations of what the trust could achieve. The local authority wanted to and was able to transfer property risks to small trusts which it created and the trust accepted these because it also thought that the there was a benefit in a long lease and a long relationship. In reality, these relationships fetter the flexibility of a local authority often tying them into poor value for money service relationships.

The trust has to be funded by the local authority to carry out repairs either through the revenue payments or via a capital grant because there is no other realistic option. It was mistakenly thought by some that new trusts could use the security of the lease to borrow against and that the trust should take on these full or very significant repairing obligations allowing the local authority to offload property risks. It has become clear this was not feasible or taxation efficient (see chapter 11) especially for a business with no assets. A new business, reliant on one funder, which usually required a significant subsidy and no track record was (and is) not attractive to conventional funder without a local authority guarantee. Funding the trust to carry out property repairs is an inefficient use of the local authority's resources.

An alternative approach of a borrowing or 'partnership' model with a private sector provider was developed and is used to this day. This is a turnkey operation of funding, building and in some instances supporting delivery was and is very costly and may require the relevant local authority to accept ultimate liability for the trust's liabilities.

The experience of the last twenty-five or thirty years has allowed there to be evidence-based understanding of the most service and cost effective property models and the most effective commercial and service drivers. It is now possible to identify the commercial and legal models and their terms and conditions which provide the optimum solutions for various options.

Restrictive Covenants and other title matters

As identified in chapters 1 and 2 some local authority leisure and recreation land was acquired many years ago. It may be subject to restrictive or other covenants whether or not it is held as charitable land. The National Playing Fields Association, known as the King George V Fields in Trust is a particular example of a charitable organisation which restricts use of land where it has supported its purchase by a local authority. This charity was set up after the death of King George V to protect parks and open spaces and donated land for the purchase of this land to be held in perpetuity as open space land, although in some instances it does have a leisure centre built on part of it. Whilst land is managed by local authorities it cannot be disposed of nor built on without the consent of this charity.

There are other examples of where some land in a local authority's portfolio either held subject to a charitable trust or where there are restrictive covenants affecting disposal powers.

The practical implication of the above is that where consent is needed it may be a relatively lengthy process and ought to be commenced at an early stage in a project.

Property Drivers

There are some key property drivers. The most important is taxation efficiency. NNDR and VAT are considered in chapter 11. Also important is a transfer of responsibility for the day-to-day management of the buildings to the contractor/provider. The local authority will retain some statutory responsibility such as health and safety, though it is the provider who has management control in order to deliver the services. These drivers support the most common disposal approach. This is a lease of all indoor premises to the new provider. The terms of the lease pass sufficient control to the provider/lessee to achieve rateable occupation. The lease sets out the parties' respective property responsibilities,

There are exceptions to this model, for example if the facility is dual use or owned by a charity (see below).

Property Structures and Drivers for Education Buildings

There are a number of reasons why the property arrangements for school facilities are different to the property arrangements for local authority owned community facilities. The most obvious is that the premises are under the control of the school not the local authority. The premises are likely to be on land which is school land, the community facilities may be dual or joint use so that the community only has use evenings, weekends and holidays use and the school may already be accessing NNDR relief. Many of these buildings were built forty to fifty years ago and are now aged, not fit for purpose and the original agreements for their build is coming to an end.

In England, changes to the structure of education mean that most schools are now run by statutory charities, such as an academy trust, free school or multi-academy or a more general educational and child focussed charity. There are also longstanding charitable trusts where a local authority runs the community or dual use leisure facilities and/or where the local authority is the sole trustee. If the school is already a statutory or other charity, the facility will already obtain NNDR relief because of its charitable status. These relationships ought to be identified within dual or joint use agreements and other management arrangements.

In local authority areas in England where there is two tier local government these dual or joint use agreements may well be tripartite with the County Council responsible for property repairs and possibly utilities. The NNDR, boilers and meters for utilities may not be separate for the leisure facilities so the payment for these may be split between the three parties based on historic usage percentages, which may be the source of tension because it is thought that the school is paying less than they ought to pay. These historic arrangements may mean that the only viable option is for the local authority to retain payment for all repairs, maintenance and utilities. This does not give the provider any incentive to be frugal.

In some instances the school and the leisure centre are physically separate, in other older facilities users require access to school land to access the facility. This is a matter of considerable concern in view of safeguarding requirements. Which party physically controls the opening, closing and daily management differs from school to school.

In Wales (where the education system is different) or in England where the school is still a maintained school NNDR is payable and no NNDR relief is achievable unless sufficient control is able to be transferred to the leisure contractor to achieve rateable occupation. Detailed consideration of factors such as whether the leisure premises are separately rated (or able to be separately rated), what the majority of their use is and who opens and controls them will be required to achieve the most NNDR beneficial structure. It may not be possible to achieve any NNDR relief. There is some old case law which suggests that a licence may be enough to allow for NNDR relief to be granted but this is potentially controversial.

It will be seen that in practice there are many differing models and relationships. The majority of these relationships are to a lesser or greater extent based on custom and practice. Some work well, others less well.

To conclude on this section, consideration of how to specify and structure the most beneficial arrangements for dual or joint use land ought to be discussed early in any project to ensure that it does not cause end of project difficulties.

Outdoor Facilities including Car Parks

There will be little or no NNDR for outdoor leisure services such as management of a park or of the playing fields, pavilions within a park and/or facilities only open in the summer for example paddling pools. Disposal of public open space land will require prior advertisement and consideration of responses. There may also be restrictive covenants making a lease difficult or complicated to achieve.

A management arrangement is likely to be preferred. This is particularly true if responsibility for the management of the park is split between a separately procured grounds maintenance company and the leisure contractor. Whilst legally, this ought not to be a complex issue, in practice arrangements for parks can cause commercial difficulties for example, in relation to repairs and maintenance for the buildings in the parks. Playing fields, the changing pavilions, paddling pools and the toilet facilities required to use them effectively can be high maintenance with limited or no income and limited ability to manage use at an affordable cost. The local authority may not wish to spend the capital to repair these and the contractor not want to be responsible for them if they could be unsafe. It is therefore essential to consider these ancillary services and activities at an early stage in any project as they are not always easy to resolve.

Car parks also ought to be mentioned. Sometimes they are an ancillary part of a leisure centre, only used by the leisure centre and can be part of the leased land. In other instances they are designated car parks and/or used by schools, an adjoining park or the public (where they are in a town centre location), with tensions about use especially at times of maximum pressure. Issues such as who controls, manages and maintains these, the impact of car parking orders with charging on usage of the leisure centre or even what happens if some or all of the car park land is redeveloped reducing the availability for leisure centres are pressure points. The local authority may wish to reserve its ability to re-develop or manage as part of a car parking order. The best approach may be a separate licence for each of these terminable on notice or for preference inclusion within the contract via management arrangements.

Any management arrangements can be included as a schedule to the contract. Early consideration of car park issues is also recommended.

The Lease

In this section the lease structure and content is considered in outline. If the land remains leisure and culture land a lease rather than a freehold disposal is the most sensible approach even where there is a community asset transfer. A lease enables the local authority to recover its assets at the end of the contract or where there is a community asset transfer if this fails to achieve its objectives. It is out of scope to consider the approach if the property is designated as surplus to requirements and has been appropriated out of leisure use (even where the planning use may include leisure).

The suggested provisions for a lease are considered in outline below:

One lease for each premises or more than one lease for the whole portfolio: experience has shown that it is far better practice to have a separate lease for each property. There are some examples, particularly historic examples where local authorities have granted a single lease for a portfolio. It may appear attractive to save time, cost and work to have one lease for more than one premises or facility particularly if all of the terms will be similar. This is a false economy because it is an inflexible model which means that if the portfolio changes a surrender and re-grant is needed which may require consideration of legal issues such as whether the test in section 123 LGA has been met for the new lease. An example of where this may be prudent if a facility is uneconomic because of financial stringency, for example the need for expensive and not cost-effective repairs, it may be taken out of the contract during the contract period. The effect of COVID-19 may speed up the process of portfolio review as social distancing requirements may make it impracticable and/or very costly to run a facility.

Rent: a peppercorn lease, otherwise known as a non-business lease provides a local authority with optimum taxation benefits (see chapter 11). In addition to this, it allows for all financial payments from the provider to be set out in the contract. It is the simplest model to have all payments in one place. To have a lease with a rent and a contract which also has payment terms is confusing, making it more difficult to carry out a transparent financial analysis of the bids. In addition, any sums which are required to be paid to the local authority will be taken into account by the bidders in their bid calculations. The only exception to this model is where there is no associated contract and the lease will be the only continuing document (apart from any transitory transfer agreement) which governs the relationship. In this example, there may be a rent paid by the contractor if the leisure centre(s) are run at a profit or a lease at a peppercorn with the local authority paying the provider under a parallel grant agreement.

Lease length: a well drafted lease will be coterminous with or for a longer period than an associated contract. If the contract is for an initial period with an extension provision the lease should be for the potentially full contract term with break provisions ensuring that it ends earlier if the contract is not extended or if the contract ends even earlier for any reason. The easiest way of achieving this is to include appropriate break provisions and/or provide for automatic termination of a lease where the contract for the relevant property is terminated. The lease will need to be specifically excluded from security of tenure under the landlord and tenant act 1954 so that the break provisions can be exercised. Providing for a lease to be as long as the extended contract avoids having to enter into new leases if the contract is extended. Where a facility is in a poor state of repair or is past its optimum use date and it may neither be economic nor affordable to repair and thus enable support the continuation of service delivery, there may be a shorter lease than for other properties or more extensive break provisions to allow for a more flexible approach.

Repairing obligations: the most common model is split repairing obligations with the local authority taking most repairing obligation. This reflects the most cost-effective risk transfer and retention. Prior to COVID-19, the private sector was willing to take a full repairing lease where a leisure centre is new or nearly new without a need for significant repair in the foreseeable future. Providers are primarily service providers not property managers Whether a full repairing lease is the most cost-effective model will be part of the tender evaluation to establish whether this is value for money and the transfer of risk is commensurate with the likely enhanced cost to the local authority of seeking to transfer all responsibilities for repair. Bidders will take a conservative view of property risk for example where significant repairing requirements are transferred the market will cost on the assumption that all repairs and replacements need to be carried out within the lower end of the life cycle cost period. In practice, this may not be necessary or carried out so the local authority pays unnecessarily for these potential costs. In any event, contractor money for investment is more expensive than a local authority's borrowing or spending from revenue or capital. A local authority may have its own funds, may be able to borrow at an affordable rate and may even be able to access some grant funding. The exception to this general position is possibly for fitness equipment where the commercial leisure contractors have agreed keen prices because of their large-scale purchase or leasing requirements. The market is willing to take responsibility for replacing fitness and other specialist equipment, though it still may be more cost effective for this to be retained by the local authority. Replacement of this has a direct impact on income generation. In any event, a survey is needed prior to letting the contract as the market does not want to take buildings where risk is unknown and they will seek to ensure that the local authority carries out its repairing obligations to protect its income risk with damages payable for any losses if the building is not repaired and/or pre-transfer repairs required to be done by the local authority to ensure that the buildings are handed over in fair or good condition. This can all give rise to financial tension in view of local authorities' financial position. The survey should be included within the procurement documents. It is best practice to have this updated via a visual photo survey agreed as accurate by both parties immediately prior to the transfer to avoid disputes on pre-existing condition. If the local authority cannot commit to paying for repairs and a property becomes unfit for purpose one approach is for there to be an early break clause in the lease. The commercial implications of this will need consideration as part of the procurement.

User clause and sub-letting: issues which can cause tension between the parties is the extent to which the local authority is willing to offer freedom for the tenant to use the facility for non-core uses such as physiotherapy and/or hire it out and the extent to which there are existing uses and a facility is let subject to these. Different local authorities have different policies over political and other potentially controversial uses for example animal fairs or Sunday markets or allow alternations.

Conclusion

As identified above, the importance of the property portfolio in modelling and delivering a sound delivery model must be understood by all who of those involved in the project and its subsequent delivery. A local authority's leisure properties are intended to support service delivery and not to have an independent value. This needs to be understood.

CHAPTER TEN

HR AND PENSIONS ISSUES

Introduction

In this section the practical implications of staffing and pension issues are considered. These include the transfer of staff under the Transfer of Undertakings *(Protection of Employment) Regulations 2006 (SI. 2006 No. 246)* (as amended by the Collective Redundancies and Transfer of Undertakings (Protection of Employment) (Amendment) Regulations 2014") ("TUPE"), pension options and implications.

The law relating to TUPE and pensions is specialist and has developed over many years. There are specific issues for these services and it is these which are focussed on in this section rather than the general law relating to human resources and pensions though it is necessary to identify the general law to make sense of the issues.

TUPE transfer and future flexibility

TUPE applies to transfer employees from one employer to the new employer where there is either the transfer of a business in part or whole or there is a service provision change. Each of these types of TUPE transfers are defined in the legislation. The general position is that employees transfer by operation of law on their existing terms and conditions if they are employed by a transferor employer (as defined in the regulations) immediately prior to the transfer.

It is the current employer who is responsible for consulting and managing the TUPE process and this consideration starts from the perspective that the current employer is the transferring local authority.

It is not possible to opt out of TUPE though it may be possible to reorganise the services in the period prior to the transfer or even at the date of transfer and thus change terms and conditions and the impact of TUPE on individual employees if the reason *'(a)...is an economic, technical, or organisational reason .. provided that the employer and employee agree that variation; or (b)the terms of that contract permit the employer to make such a variation* (extract from regulation 4 (4) as substituted in 2014). This has risks though. If an employee is dismissed and the sole or principal reason for this is TUPE the dismissal is the transfer, it will be automatically unfair (see regulation 7 as substituted in 2014). In practice, early consultation with any trade union or staff representatives is essential if re-organisation is envisaged as being sensible.

The statutory definition of an 'employee' is wide and includes any person working for the transferring employer except people under a contract for services. In theory, identifying the employees employed in the direct provision of the leisure services should simple. They will usually be a discrete group who all transfer. In practice, this may not be simple.

There may be no agreed list of employees. Their terms and conditions, length of service and employment rights may not in practice, be clear. There may be significant terms which are 'custom and practice' and not written into any contracts of employment. This may be because of the way that leisure centres and other leisure services such as grounds maintenance are delivered and have developed or may be for other reasons. Some of these are seasonal and sessional services. There may be some staff who are either classified as casual personnel with no commitment by the employer to offer future work or who are on zero hours contracts with no contractual fixed pattern of work, depending on the model used by the employer. In practice they may have had established patterns of work for many years even if these are intermittent and not reflected in any written contract of employment; therefore they may have employment status and rights. It is possible to be a TUPE transferee with limited rights or to be treated as a casual or zero hours employee whilst the legal position is different. This and other issues ought to be resolved during the early pre-transfer process.

There may also be doubt about the TUPE status of more senior management staff who may be employed to manage a whole service, whereas the transferring business or activities are only a part of their responsibility. The status of support staff may be equally unclear. Support staff may spend a limited amount of their time on the leisure services and be in a different department to the leisure staff and if so, they are unlikely to transfer. However, this will depend upon a combination of the organisational structure and what has happened in practice. Whilst the commercial sector is more sophisticated in its organisation of staff into discrete business areas especially if they know that a contract will end shortly, this is not as easy for a local authority. The outcome of this is that a TUPE transfer where services may have always been in-house and structures and deployment of staff have not been planned with a service transfer of leisure in mind may be complex. There may be equal or greater complexity for a local NPDO where the majority of services are delivered for a particular local authority though some services are delivered for other parties such as a school or a different local authority.

There are a number of different approaches to deciding on whether a person is a TUPE transferee such as what is the majority of their time spent on, what aspects of their workload is the more important. Whether TUPE applies to each individual will be fact specific. Detailed consideration of the applicable law is outside the scope of this book.

It is wise for a local authority to start considering the TUPE issues as early as possible. For in-house services, lists of employees, people whose status is unclear and anyone believed not to be an employee or an employee with redundancy, pension or any other rights should be consulted. HR professionals and lawyers should be consulted early. It is also be sensible to consult trade unions and/or staff to seek their confirmation of whether their recorded terms and conditions are accurate and it is certainly sensible to consult about the proposed transfer in a detailed and open manner. In addition to the statutory issues, if there is a risk of redundancy, employees are likely to be anxious about their future and openness and regular consultation can go some way to reducing this.

Where there is doubt about whether someone falls within the TUPE list an early analysis of the legal issues is recommended. In practice there may be some people who neither wish to transfer nor want to be considered employees with a committed workplace. If for example, it is clear that there would need to be some downsizing of central support staff and a future contractor would not want to employ these staff an agreed early retirement or redundancy may be welcomed or at least accepted.

Where a service is already outsourced it is also important for the local authority to discuss the TUPE issues with the current employer at an early stage. Whilst as identified above, it is legal the responsibility of the current employer to manage the TUPE transfer to the new employer this ignores the commercial reality which is that the cost of staff is likely to be a high percentage of the revenue cost of the services and may be as much as 75% (with on-costs). When putting together the indicative current service costs for the tender process if the cost of staff and who will transfer is unclear tenders will either or both be caveated and have a premium applied for risk.

Regulation 11 of TUPE (as amended) provides for extensive information about terms and conditions to be sent by the current employer to the new employer, but this is only triggered under the regulations 28 days before the transfer date and that is far too late in a re-procurement service. All new contracts ought to include modern TUPE clauses with a contractual requirement for delivery to the procuring local authority of full pre-procurement information with regular updates and a requirement to assist in a smooth transfer of staff. Many older contracts or legal relationships do not include these. This may be because the relationship is not contractual, which is irrelevant to whether there is a TUPE transfer. Alternatively, it may be because the relationship is so old that it pre-dates the application of TUPE to public bodies or simply because the commercial implications of end of contract issues was not fully thought through.

A contractor who does not want to lose a tender may not co-operate or they may cite data protection issues. Data protection issues can usually be resolved by obtaining staff's consent for disclosure of information, if the current employer co-operates. It is in the interests of staff to transfer as part of a smooth process so in general they will co-operate.

There are specific and detailed provisions within TUPE regarding consultation (see regulations 13 – 16 as amended). A prudent employer will consult far more extensively than the statutory requirements.

Whilst it no longer applies in England, the provisions relating to a two-tier workforce still apply in Wales (see *Circular, the Code of Practice on Workforce on Workforce Matters 2014*). This provides that on a transfer of current or past local authority employees to a third party, the transferor public body should ensure that new employees are employed on terms and conditions which are 'overall no less favourable'. The caveat to this is that if the transfer was very old, prior to the first *Code* in 2003 then it will not apply to original TUPE transferees and it does not stop an employer changing all staff's terms and conditions and thus circumventing the objective behind the *Code*.

Pensions

There are two aspects to pensions, the rights of current or former transferring employees from a local authority and the rights of new employees. The Local Government Pension Scheme ('LGPS') is a final salary scheme and thus expensive for the employer compared to the alternative, a money purchase scheme.

Existing local government employees who transfer and original transferring employees (those who were once local authority employees) are entitled to retain either membership of the LGPS or a scheme offering comparable or better pension rights (see *The Best Value Authorities Staff Transfers (Pensions) Direction 2007* for England and *The Welsh Authorities Staff Transfers (Pensions) Direction 2012*). Like the two-tier *Code*, this will not apply to transfers which pre-date it so if the employees have already lost their right to a comparable pension pre-2007 or arguably 2003, the date of the *Code* this will not remain. In practice, though a number of the early transfers especially to trusts provided for all employees to have access to the LGPS so the position may be unclear on individuals' entitlement as their terms and conditions may give them this right.

It is usual for transferee organisations to seek to join the LGPS. This can either be on the basis of open admission enabling all employees to join the LGPS, whether transferees or new employees or on a closed basis on the basis of LGPS admission only for those entitled in law to LGPS admission. There are a number of practical issues such as whether staff can transfer their existing pensions on a fully-paid-up basis or whether the new employer joins from the date of the transfer and staff's historic pension entitlements are retained in their current scheme. The joining terms, valuation, procedure and treatment of the new employer will be a matter for the relevant LGPS trustees and vary depending on the way that the individual scheme is managed. It is usual for commercial contractors to join the LGPS on a closed basis.

The terms of Local Government Pension Scheme Regulations 2013 (as amended), which are the current regulations, mean that on any admission, the transferring local authority will be required to provide a guarantee or bond to the pension fund administrator to ensure that there is no loss to the pension fund at the end of the contract if the transferring employer is unable to pay any exit deficit.

Changes implementing these requirements were made to the previous regulations some years ago. There may be a few very old community transfers to NPDOs and admission agreements still in existence where this was not a regulatory requirement and the then transferring local authority did not give a contractual commitment to the LGPS to meet any exit deficit. There may be a deficit and an exit payment at the end of the contract or relationship when services transfer because the method for calculating an exit payment is intended to ensure that there is no loss falling on the pension scheme. This sum is likely to be different to and more than a payment on a going concern (i.e. continuing business) basis. These old relationships will inevitably cause tension and the pension fund will seek to obtain a commitment from the parent local authority for any such deficit which the trust cannot meet. This is a very technically difficult topic. Individual advice is required.

The LGPS is an 'opt out' scheme. This means that eligible staff are 'opted in' unless they choose to opt out. Staff ought to be notified by the pension fund administrator that they will be enrolled automatically unless they opt out. This will happen if they are employed on a permanent basis, for more than three months and earn the trigger amount (£10,000). They have to positively 'opt out' if they do not want to be a member. Whilst they may be able to 'opt in' if they do not meet these criteria, there is a practical complexity for staff who are on zero hours or casual contracts. They may in law be permanent employees who meet the criteria for being 'opted in' and if this is not done there is a breach of the regulations by the local authority. If the new employer makes these staff redundant the pension issue may be raised within any tribunal or other claim.

The likely contribution rate will depend upon the age profile of the transferring staff, whether the scheme is open or closed to employees who are not entitled under the pensions direction and their numbers and the contract length. An actuarial calculation to establish the rate is likely to be needed at a relatively early stage depending on the procurement terms. The calculation method and way that a new admission is treated may well depend upon the approach of the scheme's actuary.

Contractors are unlikely to be willing to take pre-contract or end of contract pension risk. They may not be willing to take all or any risks arising in-contract contribution rises.

Conclusion

The practical reality is that the procuring local authority will take all beginning, staff transformation (for example. re-organisation and redundancy) and end of contract employment and pension risk (for example any end of contract redundancies and pension strain). These risks and costs will be reflected in the commercial and therefore contractual terms entered into.

Like so much about this area of law, TUPE and pensions raise technical issues with very considerable financial implications. These must all be understood and taken into account as part of the procurement analysis and terms at an early stage. If not dealt with properly in a commercially pragmatic manner they can have an effect on the ability to achieve a value for money procurement or any procurement. The market has a choice whether to bid and the terms on which it bids. Early advice, and consideration of the likely TUPE and pension issues is essential in every instance.

CHAPTER ELEVEN

TAXATION IMPLICATIONS

Introduction

Detailed consideration of taxation implications are outside the scope of this book and require technical professional advice as part of any project. As identified below, they are important in structuring any project because they can have a significant impact on the cost base and therefore the benefits or losses arising from a project.

The main taxes which are relevant are:

- VAT;

- NNDR; and

- Corporation Tax.

VAT

Like so many other aspects of local authority leisure and culture, VAT is a very technical topic. It is one of the most technical parts of an already complicated topic.

The purpose of this part of the chapter is to consider the VAT implications of various relevant situations from a practical and not a technical perspective, though there will need to be some comments on the technicalities.

Part of the complexity arises because VAT is based on European law and unless and until the law is changed, the UK courts have to apply VAT in accordance with the principles decided in Europe. It should now be open to the UK government to change the law. It is currently unclear if the government will do so, although change would not be unexpected because, as identified below, the courts have given local authorities a significantly improved position in the last few years to the detriment of the Treasury.

Local authorities have an anomalous status for VAT. Provided any exempt income is 5% or less than their total supplies in any year, a local authority can recover input tax attributable to exempt supplies. Breaching this limit will generally mean that the VAT on all exempt income is irrecoverable. This can cost a local authority a considerable amount in any year especially if it is carrying out capital spend. It may be possible for the local authority to take steps to avoid a problem provided this is realised in sufficient time during the year, for example by what is known as 'opting to tax' building that it owns. This is decision with long-lasting consequences which has to be notified to HMRC with commercial implications not all of which are necessarily advantageous and should only be carried after advice has been taken.

This status and the risk of breach are reasons why a local authority lease of leisure and culture buildings are usually what are known as non-business or peppercorn leases with no money passing from the lessee to the local authority under the lease or in connection with the land which is disposed of. There is an art in drafting these leases.

As VAT calculations are complex the risk of exceeding the partial exemption may not always be realised in time. The risk of exceeding the partial exemption limit can be a particular problem where an authority has in-house leisure and culture either because services have always been delivered in-house or where there is inadvertent in-house provision for example, there is provider failure because of COVID-19 and the service ceases to be delivered by the provider. VAT issues are a reason why in the event of provider failure an urgent *Teckal* may be advisable. The *Teckal* can obtain a separate VAT registration and will be treated as independent of the local authority for VAT if properly structured.

The VAT treatment of local authority in-house leisure and culture income has been significantly changed to the benefit of local authorities in recent years because of a series of recent cases based on European law principles and case law. The first is a European case and the remainder UK cases. Prior to these, there was a VAT advantage in externalising leisure to an eligible body, namely a NPDO, which does not have to be a charity, because certain sport, physical recreation, and physical education services the activities qualified for exemption from VAT. If the NPDO charged the full sum it did not need to account for VAT to HMRC and kept the full sum. This benefit did not apply to local authorities who had to account for VAT on these services. The consequence was that the NPDO made the same charge to the public as any other body including a local authority and kept all of the income.

This more than negated the VAT disadvantages suffered by NPDOs who cannot recover all VAT on expenditure and may not even be able to register as VATable unless their relationship with third parties, for example their parent local authority is based on contract not grant. Even where they can register their VAT recovery rate may be less than 30% of VAT paid. This can be a significant financial disadvantage. The provision of support services from a third party is a VATable supply. Even where provided free the notional value needs is vatable and VAT must be accounted for. Irrecoverable VAT can be reduced by a NPDO/trust if they deliver all or substantially all services in-house.

The recent case law means (to grossly simplify a very complicated legal and taxation position) that local authorities are also treated as NPDOs for VAT purposes and can obtain the same benefit, improving their commercial position, removing any VAT advantage in externalising these activities to a NPDO (see *London Borough of Ealing v Revenue and Customs Commissioners (Case C-633/15) [2017] BVC 35* and more recently, *Chelmsford City Council v HMRC [2020] UKFTT 432 (TC)),Midlothian Council v HMRC [2020] UKFTT 433 (TC and Mid- Ulster District Council v HMRC [2020] UKFTT 434 (TC)).* The outcome is that unless the VAT disadvantages are negated by other advantages such as NNDR benefits (see below) this is a disadvantageous option.

The above focusses on leisure externalisations. Externalisation of theatres, museums and library services have their own technical implications and can be even more technically specialist and VAT inefficient than leisure because of the treatment of their income and in the case of museums and libraries lack of income. The VAT implications of a transfer of mixed services, in particular needs to be considered with care.

Even the above superficial overview is enough to demonstrate why specialist and detailed VAT advice is essential at an early stage as part of any leisure or culture project.

Non-Domestic Rates ('NNDR')

NNDR is payable by the body in rateable occupation of non-domestic premises including local authorities. The charge is payable under Part III of the Local Government Finance Act 1988 ('LGFA') by rateable occupiers of business premises and is collected by District and Unitary Councils. This is a heavily amended Act, there is other subsequent relevant legislation and it is augmented by separate legislation in Wales. It is outside the scope of this book to analyse the legislation in any depth. The objective in this section is to identify the implications of the legislation for the way that leisure and culture externalisations and contracting are structured by local authorities and the NNDR drivers for marketplace models.

There are a number of important principles, certain categories of occupiers are entitled by law to mandatory relief for premises used for qualifying purposes and may be able to access discretionary relief. Discretionary NNDR may be given either if the organisation is not entitled to mandatory relief or to augment this. To greatly simplify this topic, the consequence for a local authority of granting any relief, mandatory or discretionary, is that some comes out of the National Pool or is supported by grant (in Wales) and is not payable by the relevant local authority.

The detailed provisions relating to the financial impact for local government beyond the scope of this chapter. Until recent changes in the law all business rates were paid into a central pool and re-allocated to local authorities according to a formula. Granting mandatory relief therefore cost the relevant local authority nothing. On the other hand, discretionary relief had (and still has) a cost implication for the local authority although (with the exception of discretionary top up for charities) the vast majority of this came out of the central pool. In England, for example, since 2013, the general rule is that 50% of the cost of relief is borne entirely by the local authority and the rest comes out of the National Pool. However, technicalities such as the calculation of business rates valuation dates means it is essential for there to be an early discussion and calculation of the actual impact of any grant of NNDR relief on the local authority year on year as the actual level of benefit will be local authority specific.

Turning to the specific issues for an individual contractor; of particular relevance to this book is mandatory charitable NNDR relief of 80% because charities who are 'wholly or mainly' in occupation for charitable purposes are entitled to this relief from NNDR (section 43 LGFA) and discretionary relief to NPDOs. Whether a charity is wholly or mainly in occupation may be a complex calculation for example if the charity also runs a profit-making business which is not separately rated such as a café or retail outlet. There is no certainty on what this means and if it means more than 50% of the floor area or significantly more than this. Different authorities interpret this differently.

It is also possible for charities to be granted relief from the remaining 20% of rates which are payable and for other categories of occupiers to be granted discretionary relief of up to 100% (section 47 LGFA). Discretionary relief is in the gift of the relevant local authority. Each local authority will have its own policy on the granting of discretionary relief. This ranges from being very generous in granting up to 100% relief to an NPDO to a policy which is far more limited in extent, is on a sliding scale and depends on the turnover of the organisation and the nature of what it does – is it something that the local authority values.

NNDR relief was an important driver for local authorities as an early driver and reason for externalising these services. It is still important and has driven the legal models in the market such as for the development of service delivery by *Teckal* (controlled companies) and those of the commercial sector.

However, as the market has developed and there have been reductions in the NNDR benefit to local authorities this taxation benefit may become less and less important as the calculation of benefit is service specific and depends a number of factors. One is geography as the NNDR in some metropolitan areas is far higher especially for large leisure centres. It is much less for smaller or rural facilities or those which do not bring in income such as libraries and museums. There are now additional factors such as the added service value that can be brought to delivery by an efficient and high quality potentially national contractor, which may or may not be a charitable trust.

Corporation Tax

Corporation tax is a tax payable by most commercial incorporated entities on their profits. It is not payable by local authorities or by charities where they use their profits for charitable purposes.

The significance of the above is that where a local authority provides services in-house or externalises services to a charity, corporation tax is not payable. Where a local authority externalises to a non-charity including a *Teckal* or controlled company or to a commercial contractor corporation tax on its profits are usually payable. A NPDO may be able to obtain an exemption from corporation tax in certain circumstances, though this is treated as a very limited exemption by HMRC and is unlikely to be achievable.

It is therefore essential to structure any externalisation to a *Teckal* with care to minimise a liability to pay corporation tax. Any commercial contractor or NPDO is responsible for payment of taxes in the normal way and corporation tax will be taken into account in their bid or offer to deliver services.

Conclusion

To conclude from the taxation perspective, the preferred legal structure for a local authority externalisation, whether via an open market procurement or other model is a standard rated contract, a peppercorn or non-business lease of each building where the local authority or another non-charity is in occupation to a charity (or failing a charity a NPDO which is eligible for discretionary NNDR relief) and a structure whereby corporation taxation is minimised. The last of these is not achievable if the contractor is a commercial provider.

It is these commercial issues which underpin the structures put in place by commercial operators/contractors which are referred to in chapter 11.

Whilst taxation issues can be perceived as technical and neither understood or taken into account at an early stage of a project it will be seen from the above that early consideration of these issues is essential and there are marketplace examples of where failure to do so have created very significant financial losses.

CHAPTER TWELVE

STATE AID

Introduction

In this chapter the following will be considered:

- What is State Aid?

- The implications and current position;

- The impact of COVID.

What is State Aid and the Current Position?

State Aid means 'forms of assistance from a public body or publicly-funded body, given to selected undertakings' – i.e. any entity whose trading 'has the potential to distort competition and affect trade between member states of the EU' (Government publication on State Aid December 2012). It includes grants, loans and any other forms of subsidies.

The European rules relating to and prohibiting State Aid are in Articles 107 and 108 of TFEU and until 31st December 2020 was monitored by the European Commission in the UK. However, *The State Aid (Revocations and Amendments) (EU Exit) Regulations 2020 (SI 1470 of 2020)* came into force on 1st January 2021 and this revoked the jurisdiction of the EU over State Aid in the UK.

There are two aspects to this in relation to leisure and cultural procurements, the historic implications for any local authorities which have previously granted State Aid and the future ability of local authorities to grant subsidies. The Government has withdrawn its previous position which would have transferred the enforcement functions of the Commission to a domestic regulator (the Competition and Markets Authority) and proposes to consult on a new domestic regime. Until then, the UK will follow World Trade Organisation (WTO) subsidy rules (see

https://www.legislation.gov.uk/ukdsi/2020/9780348212570/pdfs/ukds-iem_9780348212570_en.pdf.

Reports of the deal between Europe and the UK say that the UK has agreed to abide by common principles on how state aid should work with an independent competition agency to oversee and interpret this though without a role for the ECJ. At present though, the position on the grant of state aid unclear and there is a void until there is new legislation as the WTO rules are much more limited and do not take into account domestic subsidies. This does not mean that local authorities are necessarily free to grant aid or otherwise subsidise contractors or providers.

The Impact of COVID – 19

The impact of COVID-19 has meant that a number of leisure providers have either sought or been granted or have requested State Aid grant or other funding because they are in financial difficulties. In view of the current lack of prohibition on and regulation of State Aid it could be argued that there is nothing to stop local authorities granting State Aid. I consider this view has a number of risks.

Where there is a procured contract any such payment outside the terms of the contract is arguably a payment given to circumvent the provisions in the PCR and CCR. Any such modifications which are not legally sound by virtue of the general requirements in regulations 18 and 72 of the PCR and equivalent, regulations 8 and 43 of the CCR. Therefore, any subsidy could well be considered an illegal direct award and challengeable under the remedies provisions in the relevant regulations.

In addition, local authorities are subject to general fiduciary duties, namely general common law quasi trustee duties and fiduciary duties towards their council tax payers as identified above (see *Roberts v Hopwood [1925] AC* 578). Before a local authority provides grant aid to a provider or contractor which is in financial difficulties because of COVID-19 it ought to give careful and rational consideration to whether this would be value for money taking into account all of the circumstances. These would include whether or not there might be alternative better value contractors/providers who could deliver the services, whether the provider is failing because of COVID-19, is an inefficient provider or failing for other reasons and therefore whether, taking into account that, with the exception of libraries and duties in relation to open spaces, these are discretionary services giving financial support is appropriate.

Giving aid in these circumstances could therefore be challenged under the public procurement regime, via judicial review or a complaint to the local authority's external auditor.

_____

CHAPTER THIRTEEN

PROVIDER FAILURE

Introduction

In this chapter the implications of provider failure will be considered from the perspective of the local authority. Whilst provider failure because of the pandemic is the trigger for this chapter, it also considers the impact of provider failure in general. This topic is considered from a practical not technical insolvency law perspective as it is written for local authorities who need to understand what they need to do if their provider is at risk of failure. Any local authority who considers its provider is at risk of failing or a provider who considers it is at risk of failing needs legal and other professional advice as a matter of urgency in view of the risks and implications of the situation.

Provider failure is defined for these purposes as the provider saying that they cannot continue to deliver the services because of pending or actual insolvency. In practice, the risk of failure will almost certainly be identified by the provider before the actual failure. In view of the extensive personal and professional implications of an insolvency on the company/registered society, its staff and directors no organisation wants to become insolvent and the directors should, in practice, seek to do everything possible to avoid this by resolution of any claims and debts, an orderly transfer of services and thereafter solvent winding up of the organisation. The provider will therefore inform the local authorities and any other creditors and/or organisations for whom they provide services seeking support and assistance in avoiding insolvency.

This chapter considers the legal and practical implications of a provider saying it is about to or likely to become insolvent.

What is insolvency and its Implications, an Overview?

There are two tests for insolvency, the entity cannot pay its debts when they come due and/or it has more liabilities than assets on its balance sheet. The main legislation governing the law of insolvency is the Insolvency Act 1986 together with a number of statutory instruments. This Act applies to companies and to registered societies.

When an entity is at risk of becoming insolvent then the directors or committee of management, if the entity is a registered society, have a duty to the creditors not themselves or the shareholders. Their duty is to minimise loss to creditors. They should not continue trading if this further dissipates the remaining assets Once the directors consider that the trading is taking place at a continuing revenue loss and/or they have no reasonable expectation of trading their way out of this situation they are under a duty to the creditors to put the company into administration or liquidation.

If they continue to trade at loss whilst insolvent and therefore dissipate remaining assets the directors or committee may be guilty of wrongful trading or worse and they may be personally liable.

What happens in Practice if a Provider Considers it is Failing?

In practice, there will be a number of signs that the company may be failing, for example poor trading over a significant period and/or unwillingness by its external auditor to sign off the company as a 'going concern' as part of the annual statutory audit of accounts. COVID-19 has brought this to a head for many providers because they have been unable to trade, have incurred losses because of this and may or may not be compensated by the local authority for COVID-19 losses. As identified in chapter 7 the *PPN* guidance has said that the purpose of pandemic compensation is to secure service provision not to bail out failing companies. This becomes a 'chicken and egg' situation for all as without a payment the company will become insolvent but even with a payment the local authority may be unclear if the provider will survive.

So far all or virtually all of the failures or threatened failures in this market both before and post COVID-19 have happened to providers who have one or one main local authority partner. Whilst it is possible that COVID-19 will mean more extensive failures this is the typical position. Where there is more than one main local authority or other creditor the implications are that all creditors will need to work together to agree a bail out. This will be massively difficult. The complexity is unless agreement is reached with all of the local authorities and other creditors an orderly hand over may not be possible (see below).

The first step is that the company will contact its local authority or local authorities and seek urgent additional funds to avoid imminent insolvency with a view either to agree a more permanent solution or sufficient funds for short term purposes. The implications of a permanent bail out to avoid insolvency is outside the terms of reference of this chapter.

As continuing to deliver services, pay staff and trade is likely to reduce assets a managed hand back may well be the objective. This may or may not be possible. There are two main problems for the local authority. If the company agrees terms for a hand back with one creditor local authority and the company becomes insolvent within six months thereafter any liquidator may seek to set aside the transaction because it has created a preferential position for that creditor and was carried out with that desire. This makes it risky in settling with potentially insolvent providers. The second problem is that agreeing even a temporary bail out may be at considerable cost and there may well be significant legal issues in doing so in view of the terms of the contractual or other arrangement with the provider. State aid may have to be paid by way of a grant (see chapter 12). There are limited options if a negotiated settlement is not possible. The directors or committee will call a meeting of the company which should resolve to call a creditors' meeting which can take place immediately thereafter, notice having been given at the same time as the notice of the general meeting. The notice period for these processes is a minimum of 14 days. The company may or may not trade in the interim. If it trades the directors are at risk so a short term bail out may be needed.

At the creditors' meeting a creditor will need to step forward to appoint an administrator (if the company can be rescued and sold) or a liquidator to wind it up. However, no insolvency practitioner will be prepared to act without an indemnity for costs and any liabilities. Whilst the insolvency practitioner will first take payment out of any company assets, if the company has no or very few assets, which is possible, the creditor will be liable.

If no creditor will appoint a liquidator, the official receiver is appointed. In practice, this is likely to be only after a significant delay. In the interim, the company will not trade, staff will not be paid and will be redundant and the buildings will be left as they are.

The local authority has no power to re-take possession of the facilities without a court order or a repudiation of the lease (see Enterprise Act 2002). Only a properly appointed liquidator or administrator can repudiate. Court proceedings will take months. No liquidator or administrator will continue to trade without an indemnity for costs including any redundancy costs and if trading ceases the staff are all redundant, paid basic minimum redundancy by the state in due course.

All of this is a potential disaster for a local authority as these buildings have working machinery, may have a pool which needs maintenance etc. The worst case is that buildings cannot re-open as they are irretrievably damaged. They will certainly not re-open without extensive health and safety checks,

If a liquidator is appointed, the negotiations with the liquidator may not be easy. Only after commercially difficult discussions with the appointed insolvency practitioner will A service transfer will only take place after negotiations. It is inevitable that this will not be on particularly advantageous terms and the local authority is likely to obtain no compensation or damages, instead having to negotiate with an LGPS provider about payment of contingent pension liabilities because the provider will have exited the scheme.

In practice, in view of the above local authorities have always managed to agree arrangements with their provider partners to avoid an insolvency although some providers have thereafter become insolvent.

Continuing with Service Delivery

The wider question for the local authority will be how to continue with service delivery after their current provider hands back the services. The local authority is unlikely to have the capacity or resource to continue with service delivery without considerable cost and other difficulties. The options will all be unpalatable unless the failure comes towards the end of the procurement of a new service and there is a new contractor ready to take over.

Otherwise, the options will be to take the services in-house and seek urgent temporary expert support in putting together the required infrastructure, agree an emergency contract with a contractor under the PCR, as a below threshold CCR contract or urgently set up an *Teckal*. The second and third of these options may at least have the potential to provide some NNDR relief whilst longer term service plans are made for delivery and avoid the risk of the local authority exceeding its partial exemption limit.

All of these options will require expert advice, which should be obtained as a matter of urgency at an early stage in the discussions with the provider.

Conclusion

Provider failure or the risk of this are likely to be very expensive in the medium to longer term especially as COVID-19 is likely to make it impossible to achieve an equally good commercial service contract as available before the pandemic.

CHAPTER FOURTEEN

OVERALL CONCLUSION

Leisure culture, museums and libraries are all services which are seen as very important by local authorities and the communities that they serve even though most are not statutory services. There has been a flourishing, very successful and relatively stable mixed economy for thirty or so years with in-house delivery, the commercial sector, trusts and some *Teckal* companies existing side by side. Services and their delivery have been developed and improved, many millions have been saved via intelligent procurement and other externalisation offering a variety of established delivery options for local authorities over around the last 30 years. Prior to COVID-19 many leisure facilities operated close to or at their maximum. Recent commercial deals were based on increasing throughput and income via very busy leisure centres functioning as near to full capacity as possible with extensive fitness and other income generating activities being the driver for growth were well established.

Arts, museums and libraries have not generally not been as commercially robust as commercial leisure providers and many local authority created trusts have also been struggling for many years.

Whilst a successful market, this has never been a market which has been massively profitable for any providers. The significant period of closure of all leisure and cultural facilities and subsequent requirement for social distancing, which may continue for months is a massive long-term disruption. Until social distancing ends some leisure will are not be able to open because of their design.

The National Leisure Recovery Fund launched on 14 December 2020 in England and with a value of £100m targeted at supporting local authorities with outsourced providers is generally considered to be too little and too late.

In addition, it is unclear how far and how quickly the market and therefore providers will bounce back. It is considered by some industry experts that it will bounce back and within 18 months after normal service delivery can be resumed income will be back to normal. Even if there are only limited provider failures and previous usage and income streams return providers will need to rebuild their commercial strength and resilience as COVID-19 has tested the commercial resilience of all providers even the most robust. A few trusts have already failed and it is unclear whether more, especially smaller trusts will do so with a marketplace reduction in providers particularly smaller trusts seen as inevitable.

The longer-term commercial implications of COVID-19 on the terms achievable as outcome of new or refreshed procurements is unknown. It is unclear how far the commercial terms, acceptance of risk and bid prices offered by the market will be significantly less good for local authorities, though the *Westminster* case is likely to result in contractors being more cautious in the commercial terms which they will accept. In any event, hard pressed local authorities will need to review the affordability of these services in general and individual smaller less viable facilities in particular to focus on a few more cost-effective facilities and services. There are some services which may be particularly hard hit in the longer term, particularly those with limited income generation and/or weaker marketplaces such as libraries and museums together with theatres and other cultural buildings.

In conclusion, though much is unknown at present, leisure and culture will continue even if the services, commercial and wider landscape change.

MORE BOOKS BY
LAW BRIEF PUBLISHING

A selection of our other titles available now:-

'A Practical Guide to Solicitor and Client Costs – 2nd Edition' by Robin Dunne
'Constructive Dismissal – Practice Pointers and Principles' by Benjimin Burgher
'A Practical Guide to Religion and Belief Discrimination Claims in the Workplace' by Kashif Ali
'A Practical Guide to the Law of Medical Treatment Decisions' by Ben Troke
'Fundamental Dishonesty and QOCS in Personal Injury Proceedings: Law and Practice' by Jake Rowley
'A Practical Guide to the Law in Relation to School Exclusions' by Charlotte Hadfield & Alice de Coverley
'A Practical Guide to Divorce for the Silver Separators' by Karin Walker
'The Right to be Forgotten – The Law and Practical Issues' by Melissa Stock
'A Practical Guide to Planning Law and Rights of Way in National Parks, the Broads and AONBs' by James Maurici QC, James Neill et al
'A Practical Guide to Election Law' by Tom Tabori
'A Practical Guide to the Law in Relation to Surrogacy' by Andrew Powell
'A Practical Guide to Claims Arising from Fatal Accidents – 2nd Edition' by James Patience
'A Practical Guide to the Ownership of Employee Inventions – From Entitlement to Compensation' by James Tumbridge & Ashley Roughton
'A Practical Guide to Asbestos Claims' by Jonathan Owen & Gareth McAloon
'A Practical Guide to Stamp Duty Land Tax in England and Northern Ireland' by Suzanne O'Hara
'A Practical Guide to the Law of Farming Partnerships' by Philip Whitcomb

'Covid-19, Homeworking and the Law – The Essential Guide to Employment and GDPR Issues' by Forbes Solicitors

'Covid-19, Force Majeure and Frustration of Contracts – The Essential Guide' by Keith Markham

'Covid-19 and Criminal Law – The Essential Guide' by Ramya Nagesh

'Covid-19 and Family Law in England and Wales – The Essential Guide' by Safda Mahmood

'A Practical Guide to the Law of Unlawful Eviction and Harassment – 2nd Edition' by Stephanie Lovegrove

'Covid-19, Residential Property, Equity Release and Enfranchisement – The Essential Guide' by Paul Sams and Louise Uphill

'Covid-19, Brexit and the Law of Commercial Leases – The Essential Guide' by Mark Shelton

'A Practical Guide to Costs in Personal Injury Claims – 2nd Edition' by Matthew Hoe

'A Practical Guide to the General Data Protection Regulation (GDPR) – 2nd Edition' by Keith Markham

'Ellis on Credit Hire – Sixth Edition' by Aidan Ellis & Tim Kevan

'A Practical Guide to Working with Litigants in Person and McKenzie Friends in Family Cases' by Stuart Barlow

'Protecting Unregistered Brands: A Practical Guide to the Law of Passing Off' by Lorna Brazell

'A Practical Guide to Secondary Liability and Joint Enterprise Post-Jogee' by Joanne Cecil & James Mehigan

'A Practical Guide to the Pre-Action RTA Claims Protocol for Personal Injury Lawyers' by Antonia Ford

'A Practical Guide to Neighbour Disputes and the Law' by Alexander Walsh

'A Practical Guide to Forfeiture of Leases' by Mark Shelton

'A Practical Guide to Coercive Control for Legal Practitioners and Victims' by Rachel Horman

'A Practical Guide to Financial Ombudsman Service Claims'
by Adam Temple & Robert Scrivenor

'A Practical Guide to Advising Schools on Employment Law' by Jonathan Holden

'A Practical Guide to Running Housing Disrepair and Cavity Wall Claims:
2nd Edition' by Andrew Mckie & Ian Skeate

'A Practical Guide to Holiday Sickness Claims – 2nd Edition'
by Andrew Mckie & Ian Skeate

'Arguments and Tactics for Personal Injury and Clinical Negligence Claims'
by Dorian Williams

'A Practical Guide to Drone Law' by Rufus Ballaster, Andrew Firman, Eleanor Clot

'A Practical Guide to Compliance for Personal Injury Firms Working With Claims
Management Companies' by Paul Bennett

'A Practical Guide to Dog Law for Owners and Others' by Andrea Pitt

'RTA Allegations of Fraud in a Post-Jackson Era: The Handbook – 2nd Edition'
by Andrew Mckie

'RTA Personal Injury Claims: A Practical Guide Post-Jackson' by Andrew Mckie

'On Experts: CPR35 for Lawyers and Experts' by David Boyle

'An Introduction to Personal Injury Law' by David Boyle

'A Practical Guide to Subtle Brain Injury Claims' by Pankaj Madan

These books and more are available to order online direct from the publisher at www.lawbriefpublishing.com, where you can also read free sample chapters. For any queries, contact us on 0844 587 2383 or mail@lawbriefpublishing.com.

Our books are also usually in stock at www.amazon.co.uk with free next day delivery for Prime members, and at good legal bookshops such as Wildy & Sons.

We are regularly launching new books in our series of practical day-to-day practitioners' guides. Visit our website and join our free newsletter to be kept informed and to receive special offers, free chapters, etc.

You can also follow us on Twitter at www.twitter.com/lawbriefpub.

Printed in Great Britain
by Amazon

75924342R00086